Cambridge Elements ☰

Elements in the Philosophy of Religion
edited by
Yujin Nagasawa
University of Birmingham

GOD AND MORALITY

Anne Jeffrey
University of South Alabama

CAMBRIDGE
UNIVERSITY PRESS

University Printing House, Cambridge CB2 8BS, United Kingdom

One Liberty Plaza, 20th Floor, New York, NY 10006, USA

477 Williamstown Road, Port Melbourne, VIC 3207, Australia

314–321, 3rd Floor, Plot 3, Splendor Forum, Jasola District Centre, New Delhi – 110025, India

79 Anson Road, #06-04/06, Singapore 079906

Cambridge University Press is part of the University of Cambridge.

It furthers the University's mission by disseminating knowledge in the pursuit of education, learning, and research at the highest international levels of excellence.

www.cambridge.org
Information on this title: www.cambridge.org/9781108469449
DOI: 10.1017/9781108567701

© Anne Jeffrey 2019

First published 2019

A catalogue record for this publication is available from the British Library.

ISBN 978-1-108-46944-9 Paperback
ISSN 2399-5165 (online)
ISSN 2515-9763 (print)

God and Morality

Elements in the Philosophy of Religion

DOI: 10.1017/9781108567701
First published online: April 2019

Anne Jeffrey
University of South Alabama

Author for correspondence: Anne Jeffrey ajeffrey@southalabama.edu

Abstract: This Element has two aims. The first is to discuss arguments philosophers have made about the difference God's existence might make to questions of general interest in metaethics. The second is to argue that it is a mistake to think we can get very far in answering these questions by assuming a thin conception of God, and to suggest that exploring the implications of thick theisms for metaethics would be more fruitful.

Keywords: theism, moral value, moral obligation, normativity, moral epistemology, moral motivation

ISBNs: 9781108469449 (PB), 9781108567701 (OC)
ISSNs: 2399-5165 (online), 2515-9763 (print)

Contents

1 Introduction

Philosophical questions about God's existence – that is, theism – intersect questions in moral philosophy at a wide range of points. We can ask questions about God and applied ethics: *If God created the world, how should we treat the environment and other animals?* We might wonder whether theism is equally compatible with all normative ethical views: *If theism is true, is hedonism probably false?* Theism might also affect our metaethics – for instance, *Are moral obligations grounded in divine commands?*

In this short Element we'll consider whether theism makes a difference in answering questions of general interest in metaethics: What grounds moral truths and the normativity of morality? Do we have moral knowledge, and if so, how? What explains the rationality of moral motivation and other practical moral attitudes?

We'll canvass and evaluate major arguments in contemporary literature that take a stand on whether theism impacts or provides unique answers to these questions. While we'll limit the discussion to metaethics, the answers provide something in the way of guidance for thinking through questions downstream in normative and applied ethics. Should moral normativity be grounded in God's commands, for instance, then our evidence about the content of those commands will constrain and inform the account of which actions, in particular, are morally required or prohibited.

Contemporary debates about God and morality treat traditional theism and atheism as the major fault line along which answers fall (Adams, 1999: 5–6). Little is said about the referent of theism or God in this literature except that God is omnipotent, omniscient, and omnibenevolent – that is, the omniGod – or that "God" refers to the divinity of the Abrahamic traditions (Adams, 1999: 6; Bergmann, Murray, and Rea, 2011: 2; Evans, 2014; Hare, 2015: 3; Murphy, 2017: 2–3; Nielson, 1973: 2).

One of the most important and influential works on the topic in the last decades, Robert Adams's *Finite and Infinite Goods*, opens by clarifying that the moral framework presented is meant to be ecumenical among Christianity, Judaism, and Islam:

> Its author is a Christian, but it is not a Christian book or a study of Christian ethics. It doubtless bears in various ways the impress of my own moderately liberal Protestant beliefs, but the framework presented here is intended to have room in it for other forms of theistic ethics, including forms of Jewish and Islamic as well as Christian ethics. (Adams, 1999: 6)

Others take theism to be slightly more expansive. John Hare notes in the outset of *God's Command* that his account is felicitous to faiths including "Judaism,

Christianity, and Islam ... the Baha'is, the Druze, and many others" (Hare, 2015: iii). Even those who oppose theistic accounts of morality typically take their target to be the God of Abrahamic religions or the omniGod (Rachels, 1971). Some argue against a representative version of that God to support a generalization about all or most classical theisms (Sinnott-Armstrong, 2009). Others fail to specify the conception of God they are assuming but use various classical theisms as examples of the view they seek to refute (Mackie, 1973).

In general, the discussion operates at a remove from the substantive theistic views found in particular religions. From here on out, I call a view *thin traditional theism* (thin theism for short) if it claims no more about God than that God is the God of the Abrahamic traditions, narrowly or broadly construed, or that God is the omniGod of perfect being theology – an omnipotent, omniscient, and omnibenevolent being.

One reason for focusing on thin theism has to do with distinguishing philosophy from theology. If we presuppose a thicker conception of God, the thought goes, we end up doing theology or religious ethics rather than philosophy. Robert Adams heads off the objection that he is doing theology rather than philosophy by claiming, "The subject about which I am offering theistic hypotheses is not religious ethics as such, or any particular brand of it" (Adams, 1999: 6).

Another motivation for operating up a level of generalization is that thin theism seems like the least common denominator of clusters of specific theisms (Adams, 2006: 6). By taking thin theism as a starting point, we can paint a picture of morality mutually supported by all varieties of traditional theism. Should the account of morality be especially compelling, this strategy would demonstrate how much one can get from fairly minimal theistic assumptions.

Finally, a good philosophical argument will rest on only those assumptions needed to secure its conclusion. Thus it would make sense to steer clear of assumptions like "God is trinitarian" or "God necessarily creates" when engaged in a philosophical argument about God's relationship to morality. The question is whether thin theism really is cut out to do the work theists say it can do, or is the proper target of arguments opposing theistic accounts of morality.

We'll subject arguments on both sides to scrutiny and see that they often require more substantive assumptions about God than what is assumed in thin traditional theism. I'll suggest that, once we start paying attention to the differences such substantive assumptions make, the fault lines in the debate shift. The ensuing change of landscape puts certain thick theisms in the same metaethical territory as some atheistic and agnostic views and creates distance between them and other theisms. This approach could draw into the mainstream conversation theisms often pushed to the margins – those with origins in Eastern religions like Hinduism, Shintoism, Sikhism, and Taoism, as well as nontraditional philosophical views like pantheism and panentheism. These varieties of theism deserve a seat at the table when philosophers are discussing questions about God and morality just as much as theisms of the Abrahamic faiths.

Here is a summary of what's to come. In Section 2 we ask whether God is a metaphysical ground of morality or the normativity of morality. We'll see theists' arguments that God must ground objective moral values, moral obligations, or moral laws, as well as atheist objections to these arguments.

Section 3 turns to questions about moral epistemology. Here the arguments concern whether traditional theism implies a certain kind of moral skepticism, theistic replies to evolutionary debunking arguments against moral realism, and whether belief in supernaturally grounded moral properties is subject to special epistemic criticism.

We delve into the practical domain in Section 4. We'll ask whether certain of our moral practices and attitudes are justified only if God exists. Many of the practical arguments have the form of a Kantian transcendental argument: they attempt to show that theism is a condition on the possibility of some practical attitude or its rational justification.

Throughout, I draw attention to places where the arguments purport to rest on or target the thin traditional theism but, without further assumptions about what God is like, fail to support their conclusions. I aim to make a cumulative case not against theistic accounts of morality in general but against using thin traditional theism as a placeholder for thicker theisms in these arguments. I close by suggesting an alternative strategy for pursuing questions about God and morality: We ought to shift focus to questions about substantive conceptions of God and the grounds of morality, moral knowledge, and moral motivation and action. Foundational metaethical questions become richer, more interesting, and answers more illuminating once we thicken the conception of God under consideration. Additionally, and perhaps more importantly, our philosophical debates might make closer contact with lived religious beliefs and practices if we take this approach.

2 Grounding Normativity in God

Some contemporary theists say that God has an important role in *metaphysically grounding* morality. That is, when we ask why there are moral obligations, or laws, either their existence or their normative authority depends on God. The strong version of this metaphysical thesis says that God necessarily figures in a successful metaphysical explanation of fundamental moral truths. The moderate thesis says that God actually figures in such an explanation, though not necessarily. The weak thesis says only that God possibly figures in such an explanation.

Broadly speaking, there are two forms of argument that support different versions of the metaphysical thesis (Murphy, 2011). Data-driven arguments (what Murphy calls *explanandum-driven* arguments) take some phenomenon and show that the only thing that could explain the data, or the thing that best explains the data, is x. If we can't dismiss the phenomenon as a mere fiction and it really requires explanation, then we should believe that x exists and grounds the phenomenon. Suppose we are hiking in Colorado and observe large tracks and scat. Given the shape and size of the tracks and scat, we eliminate animals like mountain lions and marmots as responsible for them, and, given the sorts of animals that live there, we rule out various types of bear and figure that the best explanation for the tracks and scat is that a mature black bear has been walking ahead of us. By contrast, explainer-driven arguments (what Murphy calls *explanans-driven* arguments) take for granted that something exists and shows that, as it is essentially the sort of thing that must ground some phenomenon, it does ground that phenomenon. For instance, if we were to see a black bear lumbering ahead of us on a hike, and in front of us we see fresh bear tracks, we would conclude that the bear was responsible for them because it is essentially the sort of thing that leaves tracks. We wouldn't need to eliminate all other possible explanations to draw the conclusion.

Data-driven arguments for theistic accounts of morality succeed when they persuade us that there is some moral phenomenon whose existence or character requires an explanation, and that God's being responsible for the phenomenon best or uniquely explains that data. Explainer-driven arguments for the same conclusion succeed when they show that God is essentially the sort of being that must ground the moral phenomenon presented as data.

Data-driven arguments have dominated the scene in debates about God and morality. The first three arguments we'll consider for the metaphysical thesis follow the data-driven schema:

(1) There is some moral phenomenon or truth M that needs an explanation.
(2) God's metaphysically grounding that phenomenon or truth is the only or best explanation of M.
(3) Therefore, God metaphysically grounds M.

Prominent versions of this argument differ in what the phenomenon M is: objective moral value, moral obligation, and moral goodness. We'll look at each version and objections in turn, and then look at the only explainer-driven argument in the literature. We'll see that how these arguments fare often depends on the details of the theism being defended.

2.1 The Argument from Objective Moral Value

A common argument for the strong thesis is what we'll call the Argument from Objective Moral Value (Wainwright, 2005: 49). It's not just philosophers who are drawn to this argument. As C. Stephen Evans (2018) puts it, "if someone believes that morality is in some way 'objective' or 'real,' and that this moral reality requires explanation, moral arguments for God's reality naturally suggest themselves." We find this kind of argument in the philosophical literature as well as in popular texts (e.g., Craig et al., 2009: 29–31; Lewis, 1952).

Generally, the Argument from Objective Moral Value runs as follows:

(1) Morality consists of objective moral values whose existence stands in need of explanation.
(2) God's existence grounding objective moral values is the only or best candidate for explaining their existence.
(3) Therefore, God grounds objective moral values.

Some theists support (2) by claiming that if human concerns or interests, or particular human commitments and desires, grounded moral values, they would fail to ground moral values that are objective in the right way. The datum that *objective* moral values exist is supported by the phenomenology of moral disagreement. If moral values were grounded in particular human desires, commitments, or concerns, then they would be subjective. But when people disagree about subjective matters, the disagreement tends not to be as vehement or people as unyielding as when they disagree about objective matters. Yet moral disagreement is vehement, and people on opposing sides of such disagreements are unyielding (Lewis, 1942). Moreover, the appropriate way to settle disagreements that rest on subjective preferences or personal commitments is typically to step back from our partial point of view and seek an impartial solution. If we disagree about whether we should watch *RGB* or *Han Solo*, it's fine for you to act contrary to your preference and come see *RGB*. Not so with moral disagreement (Enoch, 2011: 112). If you and I are physicians and we disagree about the value of life on a ventilator, it would be morally spineless for me to seek a compromise and unplug our patient on a ventilator simply because you think we should, even if I think doing so would fail to respond appropriately to the value of the patient's life.

Even if moral values were grounded in commitments or ends common to all humans, some theists think the resulting moral system wouldn't fit the data. Some kind of morality could have evolved or been constructed by social arrangements of humans, but these theists say that such a moral system would fail to have the normative force of objective morality – that feel of inescapable, binding authority (Craig, 2003: 18). One could always play the Hobbesian fool, and, not caring about complying with human social norms, fail to feel the force of morality (Scanlon, 1998: 53; Shoemaker, 2000: 345). Additionally, a system of morality grounded in human commitments or concerns could be objectionably speciesist, giving priority to human lives over those of nonhuman animals simply because the system is structured by parochial human ends (Craig, 2009). If genuine moral objectivity excludes such species bias, then a moral system based on human interests, even universal human interests, could fail to be adequately objective. This assumes that principles based on human concerns won't be based on a concern for any beings that share a human feature such as being sentient (Morriston, 2012: 260).

While many theists focus on supporting (2), the argument only gets off the ground by granting that objective moral values exist and require explanation (1). But there are several ways to resist this assumption. One could deny that objective moral values exist, that moral values demand further metaphysical explanation, or that moral values are objective. Subjectivists and relationalists take this last strategy, but those who reject the datum in (1) this way shoulder a hefty burden of proof; they have to give us reasons to reject the commonsense conception of moral values and to adopt their revisionary conception. For present purposes, then, we'll sidestep subjectivism and address objections to (1) that accept the analysis of moral values as objective.

2.1.1 The Argument from Queerness and Error Theory

To object to the first premise by denying the existence of moral values is to take the hard road. Acceptance of not just the concept of objective moral value, but the existence of such values is deeply entrenched in beliefs and practices. We'd need a powerful argument to show that we're systematically mistaken that such values exist. And this argument would need to be accompanied by what philosophers call an error theory – a story that explains how such systematic error could have come about. J. L. Mackie and, more recently, Jonas Olson have developed the Argument from Queerness and an accompanying error theory to unsettle our confidence that objective moral values exist. If compelling, the argument and error theory give us reason to reject (1).

The error theorist begins with the same conceptual claim the theist makes: if moral values do exist, they are objective and binding. She then shows that, historically, moral objectivity is conceived of as categoricity: "Moral facts are or entail facts about categorical reasons (and correspondingly that moral claims are or entail claims about categorical reasons)" (Olson, 2011: 62). Olson says a categorical reason is a reason a person has to perform some action irrespective of whether doing so would promote the satisfaction of her aims, desires, ends, or the fulfillment of some role she occupies, or abide by the rules of some game or activity in which she engages. This is quite a strong characterization of categorical reasons, but there are others on offer – for instance, reasons that are independent of particular individuals' desires, commitments, or ends (Shafer-Landau, 2003).

The error theorist then raises a metaphysical problem: nothing in our world answers to the description of a categorical reason. Nothing is at once so authoritative as to determine that we ought to perform an action and so objective as to be independent of facts about our ends or aims. If there were such a thing, it would be too odd to warrant belief. Ordinary reasons for action – the nonmoral ones – depend on such facts: the reason for the chess player to move her bishop diagonally depends on the rules of the practice of chess and her desire to win; the reason a father has to bake his daughter a cake is because he has the end of making her happy and a cake will make her happy. If objective moral values are or entail the existence of categorical reasons, and the existence of categorical reasons is dubious, we shouldn't believe there are objective moral values.

Finally, the error theory states that our moral practices and beliefs about moral values merely developed and became entrenched to give us social and evolutionary advantages. Treating values such as the value of human life as though they are objective helps to encourage motivation to adhere to these values. So, more advantages might have been conferred on groups of humans that treated such values as objective, explaining the prevalence of these beliefs in the human population (see Section 3.2.1).

The Argument from Queerness spells bad news for the proponent of the Argument from Objective Moral Value. For if it works, there would be no special class of things (objective moral values) for God to ground, and so theism wouldn't be the only or best explanation of the datum.

To respond, theists can appropriate responses to the Argument from Queerness given by secular nonnaturalists who believe in objective moral values. These philosophers point out that the error theorist's objection relies on the notion of something's being too metaphysically "queer" to believe in. We need more clarity, they say, on what metaphysical queerness is. The error theorist owes us an account of metaphysical queerness that shows why it's so damning a property as to be the sort of thing that couldn't plausibly be instantiated. If no account of metaphysical queerness of this sort is forthcoming, so much the worse for the error theorist's objection to (1).

Consider three potential accounts of metaphysical queerness that won't support the error theorist argument (Morton and Sampson, 2014). "Queer" can't mean nonnatural, because if it did the argument would beg the question against the moral nonnaturalist. It can't be that the property "queer" picks out whatever intuitively seems odd, since moral nonnaturalists disagree with the error theorist's intuition that objective moral values are odd. Neither can "queer" mean *sui generis*, since other kinds that are *sui generis* – physical facts, for instance – obviously exist and warrant our belief in them.

The "last bulwark" construes the Argument from Queerness as an argument from parsimony. Here's a global parsimony principle: "Generally speaking, nature is simple, so simpler theories are more likely to be true" (Morton et al., 2014). Here's another, construed in probabilistic terms: "Pr(E|Error Theory) > Pr(E|~ Error Theory)" (ibid.).

What evidence could favor the error theory over the theistic theory using these parsimony principles? Ordinary moral discourse and practice doesn't seem likelier on error theory than on the view that there are objective moral values. Similarly, error theory wouldn't make the fact that evolution has shaped our commitments and talk about morality any likelier. It just suggests different implications of this fact. The two best pieces of evidence we have regarding objective moral value don't favor error theory. Thus, even the parsimony version of the Argument from Queerness fails.

If the theist uses this secular response, she has to show that her theory of objective moral value is simpler, or likelier given the evidence, than error theory. Perhaps some theisms are simple or likely enough to make good on this claim. Others, however, will not be. If the introduction of theism comes along with new puzzles and a bigger ontology to solve them, it may well not be the case that theism plus moral realism is on the whole more parsimonious than the error theory.

For instance, to respond to the problem of how creatures can be free when God foreknows every truth, some theists hold to molinism – the view that there are true counterfactuals of creaturely freedom that specify what every agent would do in any circumstances she could encounter. This introduces a host of new entities or truths into one's theory. It would be surprising if the molinist moral realism were simpler than the error theory. In fact, comparing such a theistic view to accounts that explain moral realism using human social conventions or facts about human nature, it doesn't seem that parsimony would favor theism. This will not be the case for theisms that countenance fewer entities or only add God to the realist ontology and nothing else.

2.1.2 No Source Argument

Some philosophers resist the Argument from Objective Moral Value by denying that objective moral values, or truths about them, have to have a further metaphysical ground. This strategy obviates the need for an explanation, and so for appealing to theism in the explanation of the existence of objective moral value. We'll call arguments that use this strategy No Source Arguments (Heathwood, 2012).

Suppose there are moral truths. There are two explanatory options for any moral truth: either it has a metaphysical, propositional ground – a further truth that makes the moral claim true – or it's brute. For example, consider the truth

(1) I have a moral obligation to feed my neighbor's cat.

Surely, (1) is not a brute moral truth. Perhaps what makes (1) true is some descriptive fact plus a general moral principle:

(2) I promised to feed my neighbor's cat
(3) "If a person has made a promise to perform some act then the person has, in virtue of that, a prima facie moral obligation to perform that act," (Heathwood, 2012: 4).

A moral theory like W. D. Ross's can stop the explanation there, since it welcomes brute moral truths and counts (3) as one such truth.

We might complain that (3) is an inappropriate stopping point. For what makes it the case that my promise to feed my neighbor's cat gives me an obligation to feed the cat, but the hitman's promise to assassinate Ms. Smith doesn't give him an obligation to assassinate her? Perhaps some additional or further claim about the reason for which promises generally create obligations could explain away the appearance that the hitman has an obligation.

A theist defending the Argument from Objective Value maintains that (3) is not the appropriate stopping point – that it, too, requires a ground. God must ultimately ground truths about objective moral values. To explain (3), this theist appeals to a claim about God and a principle connecting that fact to the moral claim in (3). For instance, on Divine Command Theory (DCT), the fact that God commands a person to do x is the grounds for it being morally obligatory for the person to do x. She explains (3) via

(4) God has commanded us to keep promises

and

(5) "An act is morally obligatory iff, and because, God commands it," (Heathwood, 2012: 6).

Claim (5) represents DCT.

The No Source Argument points out that we must ask whether the further claim, (5), is a brute moral truth or has a metaphysical ground. Some divine command theorists take it to be brute. Samuel Pufendorf famously asserts that the fact that God has authority to be obeyed is on a par with axioms of mathematics, which "merit belief upon their own evidence" (Hare, 2015: 58). If it is brute, then it is a metaphysically ungrounded moral truth. For it specifies the conditions under which some moral facts obtain, just like (3); and it was in virtue of this that (3) requires a metaphysical ground. If the defender of DCT takes this route, then her view doesn't hold an advantage over the secular Rossian view that stops at (3), it seems (and we will see how one might object to (5) in Section 2.2.3).

Moreover, depending on the thick conception of God a theist endorses, she might find (5) or Pufendorf's axiom implausible. First, an epistemically rational person could fail to believe in God's authority, so it hardly seems self-evident. It also requires divine authority over creatures to be a divine perfection. But many theists think that if creation is contingent, then divine authority can't be a divine perfection because, generally speaking, conditionals with contingent truths in the antecedent aren't eligible as axiomatic truths about God (Murphy, 2002).

Other theists think (5) can be metaphysically explained by some meta principle. These theists often have in mind views about the nature of God's love, or God's intentions to speak truly or not deceive (which, of course, adds to thin theism). Imagine a theist of this sort asserts the metaprinciple:

(6) "If God declares that DCT is true, then, and in virtue of that, DCT is true," (ibid.).

The No Source Argument aims to show that this strategy is doomed to failure. What made (3) and (5) moral truths, on Heathwood's iteration of the argument, is that they state conditions under which certain moral claims are true. Yet on this criterion (6) is itself a moral truth in virtue of stating conditions under which a certain moral claim, (5), will be true. Thus (6) requires further ground. The same problem arises even if the theist offers a meta-metaprinciple to explain (6), like, "If God declares that God's declaration of DCT is necessary and sufficient to make DCT true, then it will be so." For it states a condition – namely, God's declaring that God's own declaration of DCT makes it true – under which the moral claim DCT (5) is true. So too for any further meta-meta-metaprinciple; so the regress incited is vicious.

Alternatively, the theist could stop the regress by supposing the metaphysical source of DCT (5) is God's command that we do what God commands. That is, it is the case that we ought to do what God commands because God commands that we ought to do what God commands. This obviously assumes that DCT is true – that the obligatoriness of doing what God commands rests on the obligatoriness of doing what God commands. "This circle is too tight to make for a genuine explanation," and it can't make for a good metaphysical explanation since that explanatory relation is supposed to be an asymmetrical one (Heathwood, 2012: 8).

The No Source Argument attempts to reveal this as a problem for any moral theory that identifies a final, nonmoral ground for all moral truths without infinite regress or circularity. As long as the statement of the theory is itself a moral truth, it will require a ground, and the truth that serves as its ground will state conditions under which the theory's conditions for a moral claim's truth are met, and so will be a moral truth, and so on. Thus, there are some brute moral truths that require no ground, and for which we can therefore not give an explanation. This casts doubt on premise (1) of the Argument from Objective Moral Value, since it assumes that the truth about objective moral value requires a nontrivial, informative, contained explanation – something the No Source Argument says is impossible.

The theist who asserts (6) can respond by calling into question the criterion for calling a claim a moral truth. Here is the only support we get for the criterion in Heathwood's argument: the Rossian principle that "if a person has made a promise to perform some act then the person has, in virtue of that, a prima facie moral obligation to perform that act" is a basic moral truth. This shares a structure with the principle that "if God has commanded a person to perform some act then the person has, in virtue of that, a moral obligation to perform that act." So the latter principle is a basic moral truth. Heathwood asserts that (6) also exhibits the structure of the Rossian principle, and so is a basic moral fact if true (ibid.: 7).

But accepting the criterion has implications that are too radical, so the theist can use a Moorean move to reject it. For one thing, it collapses metaethics – inquiry into second-order facts *about* ethics – into ethics. Second, it makes paradoxes of many innocuous-seeming metaethical views, like reductivist naturalism; if reductivist naturalism is true, then there are no irreducible moral facts, but if this itself is a moral fact with no further explanation, reductivist naturalism is false. Third, imagine what would be true if the criteria were generalized and used in another domain. Take a biological truth:

(1) Plants require sunlight to live.

This is made true by truths about plants, the chemical formula of NADPH and ADP, and a chemical truth about photosynthesis that states conditions under which food and energy are made by the plant:

(2) $6CO_2 + 6H_2O \rightarrow C_6H_{12}O_6 + 6O_2$

In explaining (2), we must eventually appeal to the physical processes. The observed efficiency of the energy transfer from photons to the light-harvesting proteins has to be explained by some further truth. Here physicists dispute the following claim:

(3) Energy transfer happens in P at n% efficiency because of quantum transfer.

(3) is supposed to be a physics claim, according to scientists debating it. And yet it states conditions under which some chemical reaction claim is true, and that chemical reaction claim states conditions under which some biological claim is true. According to the criteria used in the No Source Argument, all these claims become biological claims in virtue of stating conditions under which a biological claim is true. Since the criterion is implausible when applied outside the moral domain, the theist can say she has no good reason to accept it.

There is another way to run the No Source Argument without the dubious view about what makes something a moral claim, though.[1] Suppose, instead, a proposition is a moral claim just in case it specifies some factor, x, that contributes to the moral obligatoriness of certain actions.

This revised principle doesn't threaten to collapse all metaethical claims into moral, or first-order ethical, claims; for metaethical claims provide conceptual or linguistic analyses of what makes something morally obligatory without filling in which things in the world satisfy the relevant concepts or are referred to by the relevant terms. It does not specify a particular factor, x, that contributes to moral obligatoriness of an action but instead describes what concept or term x must satisfy or the semantics of moral obligation that sets parameters on what the referent of an obligation, x, might be. Since reductive naturalism is one such metaethical claim, the revised principle doesn't generate a paradox for the view.

Neither does it seem to have implausible consequences when applied to domains besides the moral. Take, for instance, the biological property of being healthy for a plant: chemical facts about photosynthesis do not specify factors that contribute to *plant health*. They specify which molecules, and in what ratios, are needed for a certain reaction that produces energy. Biological claims, by contrast, tell us that plants need energy to be healthy, or that plants can only use carbon dioxide, sunlight, and water as resources to produce energy.

---

[1] I am grateful to an anonymous referee for raising this possibility.

The revised principle is a double-edged sword. It avoids objections I've raised but won't show that DCT incites a vicious regress if the version of theism on offer supports the idea that truth is prior to goodness. Suppose what makes DCT true is that God declares it, and what goodness is depends on what is true. Now the claim that God's declaration of something makes it true is not a moral claim according to this principle. It doesn't specify which features make an action obligatory. Therefore, it is not a moral claim and will not itself require a further ground.

2.2 Arguments from Moral Obligation

Let's turn our attention to another series of arguments in defense of the strong metaphysical thesis, this time taking the data to be moral obligations:

(1) There are moral obligations, whose existence stand in need of explanation.
(2) God's will or some act of divine will grounding obligations is the best or only available explanation.
(3) Therefore God's will or some act of divine will metaphysically grounds moral obligations.

Most often, we find such in the mouths of theological voluntarists – those who defend the view that moral obligations depend on God's will or some act of divine will, such as a command (see Murphy, 2011: 100).

One such argument maintains that (2) is true because God is the necessary and sufficient cause of all moral obligations (Quinn, 1990). On this view, God is the necessary cause of moral obligations because all truths depend on God as absolute creator, even necessary truths. Whether truths about moral obligations are necessary or contingent, God, as absolute and sovereign creator, must make them true. Moreover, God does make them true: "moral facts are as they are because God has the beliefs He does about what people ought and ought not to do" (Quinn, 1990: 361). Further, God's beliefs and God's willings are one either because God is simple or they are so tightly knit that they covary across all possible worlds (ibid.: 362).

The argument above, it has been pointed out, relies on a distinction between antecedent and consequent divine willings. Antecedent willings represent God's intentions prior to consideration of all the details of circumstances and persons concerning the intentional object. Consequent willings are God's all-things-considered intentions. The reason to maintain this distinction is that if we were to say moral obligations were caused by God's consequent willings, then it would be impossible to violate moral obligations (Murphy, 1998). Since the data doesn't show that there are moral obligations that are not possible to violate, God's consequent will wouldn't be the right sort of thing to ground moral obligations. So, it has been pointed out, divine willings must be conceived of as antecedent willings so that moral obligations can express requirements with the possibility of being violated.

The proponents of this argument claim that it is open to all classical theists (Quinn, 1978: Ch. 6). Is that right? The major assumption that supports the argument is that God is necessarily the grounds of all truths, even necessary truths. This conception of God's sovereignty, though, is disputed and subject to forceful objections (e.g., Davidson, 1999). Further, the argument maintains that divine willings and beliefs covary in a modally robust way, at the least, and are identical, at best. While divine simplicity is held by some to be a divine attribute, others deny this. Nor is it clear that all theists would accept the tight connection between divine normative beliefs and divine willings; as we will see in Section 3.2.4, we can imagine God having reasons to refrain from willing something that God believes ought to be the case without rational incoherence due to some other divine purpose (Moon, 2017).

G. E. M. Anscombe's widely discussed "Modern Moral Philosophy" is often read as an argument that God must figure in the grounds of the very concept of moral obligation and "ought" (Anscombe, 1958). On this reading, Anscombe's idea is that the concepts of moral obligation and "ought" fit in a picture on which there is a moral law. In order for there to be a moral law, there must be lawgiver that meets certain conditions for having authority of the right sort. As no human being, possible or actual, could meet those conditions, we must either abandon our concept of moral obligation and turn to a secular virtue ethics, or accept again that there is a divine lawgiver.

Finally, Nicholas Wolterstorff's account of justice features a similar argument according to which the obligations arising from human rights can only be explained if some theistic fact grounds human rights (2008: chapters 15–16). God loves all human beings equally in a particular mode, or way, of loving. This love endows humans with worth. That worth and the diverse expressions of it explain the equal moral status of humans and the demands that humans can make on one another no matter how impaired they may be, which he calls human rights.

These iterations of the Argument from Moral Obligation purport to fit well with at least Christianity and Judaism. The concepts of moral law and of justice are among the central moral categories in Scripture. Moreover, we can see in both the notion that God is the lawgiver. Perhaps, then, such Arguments from Moral Obligation are the sort that will support thin traditional theism.

Take the last example of the argument first. The conception of God required to support Wolterstorff's argument requires interpretive choices of Scripture regarding the nature of justice and its centrality (e.g., Attridge 2009). It also presupposes a theological view about the primacy of the individual relationship of God to creature over the created moral order (e.g., O'Donovan 2009). Turn to the first two examples, now. Several strands within Islam and Christianity contain philosophical discussions of the law that indicate that the source of the natural law or moral law resides in *both* human reason and divine will. These views countenance the possibility that action can be obligatory but not in virtue of a divine lawgiver. The divine enters the explanation at a lower level – namely, in explaining why nature has the purposes it does and why human reason has the ability to discern good from evil. For example, in the Hard Natural Law tradition in Islam, "nature is deliberately created by a just God who creates the world to benefit humanity," and human reason has this same purpose. God endows nature with objective, discoverable good and bad qualities, and human reason with the ability to detect these qualities and then produce benefit on the basis of its judgment. The immediate grounds of an action's being obligatory are the objective benefit it confers on humanity, not divine will (Emon, 2010: 44). Contrast this with the Soft Natural Law tradition on which the coupling of natural facts with value depends on the divine mind, which can change, and so is contingent (ibid.: 124).

The Hard Natural Law example illustrates that further details about God's intentions can support or detract from the fit of theism with Quinn's and Anscombe's Arguments from Moral Obligation. If God imbues nature with a certain kind of autonomy, intending for humans to benefit one another through the autonomous use of reason, it becomes less clear that divine commands or laws are necessary to ground obligations on the theistic picture. If God immediately grounds the facts about what natural actions are beneficial and God's mind is subject to change, as the Soft Natural Law theorists claim, then it does look like the divine lawgiver plays a central, ineliminable role in moral obligation.

2.2.1 Autonomy

One objection theological voluntarists must face is based on a concern about human autonomy. The thought goes that it would be morally impermissible to violate or abdicate our own moral autonomy – that is, our making free and deliberate moral choices; but following divine commands would require abdication of or violation of our moral autonomy; therefore, divine command ethical theories must be false.

Some theists say that the autonomy objection fails because it assumes that a person must believe she is following divine commands in order to be giving up her autonomy in acting as she is obligated. But read as a theory about the grounds of moral obligations, this obviously need not be so (Evans, 2013: 95).

Someone can perform the action she is morally obligated to without knowing that the reason it is obligatory is because God commanded it or it is what God antecedently wills that she do.

To make use of this response, the theist needs to assume that God only wills that the person do what God commands *de re*, not *de dicto*. Many theological voluntarists alive to the autonomy objection do make such an assumption, as well as theists in rationalist strands of their tradition according to which moral laws or principles are discoverable by reason without divine revelation. But not all theists conceive of God as merely wanting certain actions and states of affairs to come about, even if not under the description "what God wills." We can imagine a theist arguing for the opposing view, that a person fulfills her moral obligations only if she acts for the reason that God says so, because otherwise the following scenario is possible: God commands Pauline to eat meat, but Pauline believes that God wants her to be a vegetarian; in rebellion, Pauline eats meat; Pauline fulfills her moral obligations. To get around this, a divine command theorist must assume a substantive view about what God wills – namely, that God wills for all persons that they not act contrary to conscience.

A further reply to the autonomy objection states that God's requiring that we conform our actions to God's will or commands isn't an attempt to limit our autonomy. Instead, it could allow liberal use of autonomy, and development of autonomous rational capacities, to interpret and apply very general commands (ibid.: 97–8).

This, again, will require the theist to say more about God's intentions than is supplied by thin traditional theism. The commands must be general and abstract enough to give persons ample room in applying them. This lends itself neatly to the Christian Scripture on which all the commandments and the laws can be summed up in the requirements to love God and neighbor. But theisms on which divine commands cannot be so neatly summed up, or on which God regularly gives highly specific and individualized commands don't give the agent as wide a berth, or require so much development of rational capacities, to exercise autonomy. In addition, it must not be the case on that theism that the aspiration is to become equal to God in moral understanding and ordering. Again, this is not something on which all traditional theisms agree; the Eastern Orthodox doctrine of *theosis* – believers becoming God – potentially conflicts with the DCT response. The autonomy objection could be more worrisome on that thick variety of theism.

2.2.2 The Cudworthy Objection

Let's consider one of the most infamous problems with premise (3) of the Argument from Moral Obligation. Philosophers have followed Ralph

Cudworth in claiming that the divine will or commands aren't fitting explainers for the phenomena of moral obligations, and human social facts or demands are better explainers (e.g., Darwall, 1995). This objection amounts to a rejection of the moderate metaphysical thesis.

Cudworth begins by asking under what conditions God's will might make some existing thing different from what it is. For instance, can God, by sheer act of will, make a rough sea calm or turn water to wine? Well, it depends. For any x, whether God's will can make x F depends on whether x is not-F *by nature*. If the sea were rough by nature, not even God could make it not-rough. But if the sea is neither calm by nature nor rough by nature, then God could make a rough sea calm by an act of will. If, say, water is by nature not wine, then not even God's will could make it wine. Under what conditions could God's will make an act morally obligatory, then? If an act is morally obligatory by nature, God's will can't make it not obligatory. For God to be able to make an act obligatory by God's will, the act must be morally neutral by nature (Cudworth, 1996: 18).

Cudworth takes issue with the idea that God's will could make a previously morally neutral thing either good or bad, however, because the will can't have a normative effect unless it already meets some normative condition not imposed by the will. Imagine I visit a historical residence and the proprietor demands twenty dollars to enter. It seems I'm obligated to do it. What explains the apparent obligation? It's not as though the act of paying someone twenty dollars to enter their property is *by nature* morally good or obligatory. Could what makes it obligatory in this case be that the proprietor wills it? Cudworth would say no. If the person at the door were an imposter or my toddler, the person's will would fail to make the payment obligatory. A better explanation is that a person's will generates an obligation in virtue of that person having *special standing* – a kind of authority to make it the case that I'm obligated to pay them. My toddler and the imposter lack this standing, and the proprietor has it. The fact that I am obliged to obey a person with special standing, though, isn't a fact made true by anyone's will. Thus, the will alone – not even God's – can make an act that is morally neutral morally obligatory.

The Cudworthy objection's target must be narrower than theistic accounts of moral obligation, despite the fact that it is usually used to knock down all such accounts. At best, the argument shows that God's *will* can't be the metaphysical grounds of moral obligations. However, some theists assert that God figures in the metaphysical explanation of moral obligations without God's will or commands doing that work. On divine concurrentism, for example, God's nature and the nature of creatures together select for certain moral laws for each kind of creature, which ground moral obligations for human beings. Others claim God's perfect nature grounds moral obligations (Cottingham, 2005: 49–56).

Second, the objector must assume that God's will is similar enough to ours that the argument from analogy makes sense. Again, philosophers and theologians have disagreed about how we should think of the divine will, and even whether we should attribute a will to God at all. Maimonides, al-Farabi, and Avicenna all conceive of God as willing without thought or deliberation, and say that what we describe as God's action in the world is the manifestation of God's unified essence (Pessin, 2013: 28–31). Coupled with a view of the divine essence as absolutely good, this account of the divine will provides strong reasons to resist analogies with the normative insufficiency of the wills of human beings that are psychologically fragmented and deficient in their goodness.

2.2.3 The Arbitrariness Objection

The most frequently used and apparently damning objection to theological voluntarism in general, and to premise (2) of the Arguments from Moral Obligation specifically, is the Arbitrariness Objection. The commonsense version states that, if moral obligations are divine commands, then in principle it's possible that there's a moral obligation to do things that seem horrendous, like killing one's innocent child (e.g., Isaac), as long as God commands it. This implies that certain natural properties and facts – such as the pain and suffering of an innocent child – are by themselves normatively inert (Murphy 2011, 116–120).[2] Surely any metaethical account of morality with these implications is mistaken. So God's commands can't be the sole ground of moral obligations.

How strong is this objection? And is every version of theism plus DCT equally susceptible to it? With respect to strength, not very. And certain varieties of theism and theistic accounts of obligation can avoid it altogether.

The commonsense Arbitrariness Objection stresses the repugnance of conditionals like "if God commanded killing of an innocent, then killing of an innocent would be morally obligatory." In claiming that divine commands metaphysically explain moral obligations, DCT is stuck with such repugnant conditionals. Variations among theisms with respect to divine freedom and decision, however, make a difference to available replies to this objection. For theists that conceive of divine freedom as without limits, adding a moral constraint on what God can command would impose an objectionable limit on divine freedom, therefore there are no moral constraints on what God

---

[2] I am indebted to an anonymous referee for pointing out this further reason to rely on our intuitions about actions like killing innocent children.

commands (Murphy, 2014). This view must *countenance the possibility* of God issuing such commands in order to secure their conception of divine freedom. Theists with narrower conceptions of divine freedom, however, *deny the possibility* of the antecedents of repugnant conditionals, like God's commanding the killing of innocents. For according to theists like Adams, God's excellent nature is such that God couldn't command such actions (Adams, 1999). Or on Murphy's view, God's being a perfect practical agent prevents God from willing evil, even as a means to good – God is no consequentialist (Murphy, 2017). It's metaphysically, even conceptually, impossible for a being as perfect as God to command us to kill innocents, on these views.

We might think, then, that it's better for proponents of DCT to endorse a narrow, rather than a wide, conception of divine freedom to avail themselves of this response to the Arbitrariness Objection. But as things turn out, this would require an unorthodox semantics for counterpossibles – a rich but technical topic we don't have time to explore here (though for review of this part of the literature see Miller 2013).

The Arbitrariness Objection may be an attempt to point to a conceptual tension in theological voluntarism:

(1) "Let us suppose that it is the case that there is some action A that is right (wrong) only because God wants us to do (refrain from doing) it.

(2) There must be some reason for God's wanting us to do (refrain from doing) A, some reason that does not involve God's wanting us to do (refrain from doing) it.

(3) Therefore, that reason must also be a reason why A is right (wrong).

(4) So we have a contradiction, (1) is false, and either there are no actions that are right (wrong) because God wants us to do (refrain from doing) them or, if there are such actions, that is not the only reason why those actions are right (wrong)" (Brody, 1981: 143).

Brody here draws our attention to the fact that the more constraints on God's command the theist appeals to, the less work the command is doing in specifying the obligations' content.

We can resist this form of the argument by questioning the inference from (2) to (3). Theists who embrace what I'll call a hybrid view can do just this. Let's turn to hybrid views now.

2.2.4 Hybrid Views

A hybrid view is a view on which the account of moral obligation is voluntarist but the account of moral goodness is not, and the account of goodness is prior to the account of the right, or obligation. Such a view can escape the arbitrariness objection. On such a view, there are prior facts about goodness, and God's goodness, that limit possible contents of divine commands (Adams 1999: 248). Suppose that there is some action that is excellent, and this gives God a reason to want us to perform the action (premise 2 from Brody's argument). A hybrid view can say that the reason isn't sufficient to generate a moral obligation to perform the action. God's will or command must be the grounds of the moral obligation. An additional advantage of hybrid views is that they can impose moral constraints on what God can command while preserving this important role for divine commands or will in their theory. For the view will give an account of God's goodness that is independent of, and prior to, what God commands; that goodness limits what God will demand from us, as a truly good being won't require us to perform bad acts. Let's consider two versions of the Argument from Moral Obligation made by defenders of hybrid views: the conceptual version and the social-relational version.

The conceptual version of the argument takes a cue from Scotus. The concept "God" entails that if God exists, then God is supremely good. The concept "to be loved" implies that what is supremely good is to be loved. If we synthesize our knowledge of these concepts, we can conclude that the fact that God is to be loved is conceptually necessary (Hare, 2015: 18). There are two ways of loving another – to will what the other wills, or to will what the other wills we will. Since we lack many significant features of God's, God wouldn't want us to will what God wills (wouldn't it be disastrous if a finite, limited-in-knowledge creature dealt out punishments upon those she thought were wicked?). For creatures like us, loving God must consist in willing what God wills that we will – that is, in obedience to God's will. On this view, the justification of the claim that God is to be obeyed rests on a conceptual truth, rather than on something that itself requires justification.

This argument requires that God is worthy of love from human beings as a conceptual matter. We can conceive of a God, however, whose goodness doesn't require God to promote the wellbeing of rational creatures like us, and rational creatures whose ethics requires solidarity with fellow creatures (see Murphy, 2017: 134). Philosophers in the the Ash'aris tradition such as Ibn Taymiyya maintain that it is impossible for God to love humans and be loved by humans, for "only a nonexistent or something susceptible to nonexistence can be loved" (Hoover, 2007: 72). As Murphy (ibid.) argues, refusing to side with a being that fails to promote the wellbeing of one's fellow creatures – especially a being that is omnipotent and fails to share ends with you and your fellow creatures – seems entirely reasonable, maybe even required by one's reasons. One must assume that these conceptions of divine perfection are mistaken to make use of the Scotist Argument from Moral Obligation.

The sociorelational version of the argument takes as data several aspects of moral obligation that highlight its relational nature:

(1) Moral obligations are the object of special attention and care.

(2) When someone violates a moral obligation, and has no excuse, both guilt and blame are appropriate.

(3) Moral obligations "constitute reasons for doing what one is obligated to do."

(4) The motive for complying with a moral obligation seems to involve the valuing of a social bond or relationship, instead of the motive of achieving an ideal or end.

(5) "Our reasons for complying with demands may also be affected by our evaluation of the personal characteristics of those who make them" and by "how good the demand is" (Adams, 1999: 235–244).

(6) "The role of moral obligation is partly determined by the obligations we actually believe in," and for this reason moral obligations have to be recognized (ibid.: 247).

The next part of the argument attempts to illustrate that divine commands uniquely satisfy the description of whatever plays the roles for moral obligations picked out above.

(7) The motivation for complying with God's commands comes from highly valuing one's relationship with God.

(8) Because God is supremely knowledgeable, wise, rich in perfection, we have strong reasons for complying with the demands contained in divine commands.

(9) God's supreme excellence explains why divine commands should have pride of place among our obligations (ibid.: 247–57).

Further, unlike impersonal moral rules or ideals, violations of which may make us feel shame:

(10) Violating divine commands results in our being alienated from God. This explains the onset of guilt, reasons for God to blame us, and for us to require forgiveness (257).

So

(11) Divine commands are uniquely well suited to play the role of moral obligations.

The most controversial claim among fellow theological voluntarists is the hybrid theorist's claim that God's goodness is prior to and restricts God's commands. This obviously isn't agreed upon by all theisms that are supposed to fall under the heading of thin traditional theism. Let's set aside that worry for now.

The sociorelational Argument from Moral Obligation also operates on the assumption that God is "a person, or importantly like a person" (ibid.: 42). It presumes God has features that make a relationship with God valuable enough to humans that securing that relationship provides motivation for obedience: "If God is our creator, if God loves us, if God gives us all the good that we enjoy, those are clearly reasons to prize God's friendship" (ibid.: 252). Further, God must be able to occasion guilt and alleviate it through forgiveness. Presumably, God can have emotions or reactive attitudes when we violate commands that constitute blame, generate guilt, and demand apology. Divine forgiveness, if it is anything like human forgiveness, requires some sort of change in these reactive attitudes or a choice to absolve us from due penalty. All of this requires personification of God that makes sense of emotional engagement and choice in response to what humans do.

There are varieties of traditional theism that resist the idea that God is a person or personlike in these ways. In the Shi'ite Islamic tradition, there is a live controversy about whether God is personal; some say that "God is too great to be said to have a 'self' or 'mind'" (Legenhausen, 1986: 314). Another line of thought in this strand of theism goes like this: God is not in a metaphysical category, but if God were personal or a person, God would belong to the category substance; therefore God is not personal or a person (ibid.: 318). If not every traditional theism is compatible with the view that God is a person or importantly like a person, then it doesn't look like one can make the hybrid view's version of the argument work on only thin theism.

The argument also gains plausibility from a certain view of omniscience as including knowledge of future contingent truths. Suppose there are no future contingent truths to be known by even an omniscient being. Typically, we think that a reason to do as someone demands depends on them being reliable enough in the subject that they always make demands on the basis of better information than we have. If God doesn't know the future, then there could be some cases in which the reason to do what we are morally obligated to do seems stronger than the reason to do what God commands, as the latter reason could be defeasible as God is reliable but not infallible. So, divine commands are not the same as moral obligations.

Suppose God's knowledge doesn't include subjective or indexical knowledge (see Zagzebski, 2013 and Peels, 2016). If subjective or indexical facts

(facts about what it is like to see a moral situation from my perspective) do figure in what we are obligated to do, then perhaps we are sometimes better positioned than God to make moral judgments about what we ought to do. God might have a correct belief about what we ought to do but has to rely on inferential knowledge to get there, whereas I have noninferential, indexical knowledge that gets me there. In that case we would doubt whether the reasons we have based on divine commands are stronger than reasons we have based on our own judgments.

The Argument from Moral Obligation presumes that God has intimate involvement with as many humans as have moral obligations. Divine commands have to be communicated to humans and widely recognized, and in order to alleviate guilt from violating moral obligations humans have to apologize and seek divine forgiveness. While this might fit some Christian and Jewish pictures well, not all traditional theisms hold that God is as forgiving as this picture would suppose.

Another objection levied against the Argument from Moral Obligation arises from the problem of divine hiddenness. According to this problem, God does not reveal Godself to all reasonable nonresistant nonbelievers, and God's will is hidden from them. But then the exchange of apology and forgiveness for violations of God's will or commands will also be unavailable to these non-believers (Morriston 2009). For Adams analyzes moral obligations as arising from an interpersonal relationship where apology is called for and forgiveness offered due to communication of demands as authoritative. Those nonresistant nonbelievers lack the relationship, or cannot interpret signs of God's command appropriately because they do not see supposed divine commands as author-itative or directly addressed by a personal being to them in virtue of their nonbelief. Thus they don't seem to meet the conditions for being obligated, or otherwise it seems unfair that they would be so obligated given their epistemic position (ibid.: 4, 6, 8 and Danaher 2017).

Not every version of the Argument from Moral Obligation rests on a theism that involves the sort of interpersonal relationship Adams envisions holding between God and moral agents. Evans, for instance, insists that atheists need not recognize divine commands as such in order to appreciate and respond to the moral considerations they embody (2013, 20). Moral agents don't have to understand all the deep properties of moral obligations, like where their author-ity comes from, to respond appropriately. Or God could communicate com-mands through conscience, which nonbelievers regard as having some authority or reason-giving force (Jeffrey 2015, forthcoming; Evans 2013, 114). The problem raised for this sort of view is a Nietzschean worry about the validity of the vehicle of divine commands for the nonbeliever: why not reject conscience, or social norms, as merely claiming authority and subsequent demands as illegitimate (Weilenberg 2014, 79; Blackman forthcoming).

Even the varieties of Christianity and Judaism to which the account seems friendly face a philosophical puzzle about standing to forgive, and in order to reply persuasively the theist must assume even more about the divine nature and purposes (Warmke, 2017). When we violate moral obligations in failing to give what we owe others, it looks as though we owe those others an apology for wronging them. But if (10) is correct then God has standing to forgive either because we really wrong God or God has standing to forgive on others' behalf. How is this possible? If God is impassable then God cannot be wronged. If God has indirect or third-party standing it seems that we'll have residual guilt generated by the party we wronged even when we receive God's forgiveness.

The solution suggested to this puzzle requires that God has personal care for every human being, giving God third-party standing to forgive. Further, God commands that we apologize to others even if we do not require their forgiveness apart from this command. Some theists won't be able to avail themselves of this solution, either because they deny God's necessary care for the wellbeing of all humans or because they limit the scope of those whom God personally cares for.

In sum, the argument may avoid the Arbitrariness Objection, but its scope is limited by certain theistic assumptions: God's goodness is prior to God's will and constrains divine choice and action; God has knowledge of future contingents or is reliable enough that God's commands have strong reason-giving force; God is intimately involved with and not hidden to most human beings; God can forgive all wrongdoing; and God is a person or importantly like a person.

2.2.5 Secular Contractualism

The sociorelational version of the Argument from Moral Obligation assumes divine commands are uniquely suited to play the semantically indicated roles of moral obligations. An atheist could object by showing that some secular model or entity can play the same roles. Contemporary contractualism would best fit the bill here.

On one such view, principles that reasonable persons wouldn't reasonably reject determine what we owe each other (Scanlon, 1998). Many of the claims of the theist's argument above assume that a system of human social requirements will be susceptible to possibilities such as human communities not sufficiently respecting or valuing certain individuals, failure to make appropriate demands, corrupt authority, and mistaken valuing of social bonds or persons that are not excellent, thus lacking in goodness (Adams 1999, 242–244).

However, by adding ideal reasonableness constraints on the natures of the societies and persons who can issue such demands, the contractualist can insure against these problems just as well as the theist. Further, the motivation to comply with the contractualist principles are relational, on contractualist views. Human relationships seem to be at the root of what we value. What most ordinary people in fact value presupposes the value of relationships of mutual recognition. Those who value this relationship are motivated to comply with moral requirements, "but for such a person these requirements are not just formal imperatives; they are aspects of the positive value of a way of living with others" (Scanlon 1998, 162). These considerations cast doubt on the claim that God's commands can *uniquely* play the roles indicated by moral obligation.

Here, the theist might take refuge in the moderate metaphysical thesis. While an ideal community of reasonable persons can ground moral obligations, in fact, God grounds moral obligations and we have reason enough to think so – it fits the data. Perhaps the theist can offer theism as a supplement, rather than an alternative, to contractualism. For Scanlon and other contractualists are notorious for endorsing quietism about the metaphysics of morals – the view that we can assert that there are normative and moral facts without giving a metaphysical explanation for them (McPherson, 2011). If all contractualist theories were quietist, the theist could claim with ease that theism is the only candidate for a *metaphysical* ground of moral obligations.

Whether a theism can make this move depends on how much discretion it says God gives human beings, how involved God is in setting the rules for human life, and what the connection is between human reason and the divine mind or will.

2.3 The Argument from Goodness

The final prominent data-driven argument for the strong metaphysical thesis is the Argument from Goodness. Facts about goodness must appeal to God in their metaphysical grounds because goodness is best analyzed as resemblance to God, according to this argument.

It begins with an account of what the property of goodness would be if instantiated. How to go about obtaining that account is a matter of controversy, but the Argument from Goodness takes for granted that merely analyzing linguistic use of the term "good" will do us no good. Instead, it presumes that the meaning of the word "good" in certain relevant contexts can shed light on the role(s) that the property of goodness is thought to play. This role can set parameters on what something would have to be like in order to be the property of goodness (Adams, 1999: 16–17).

In the contexts where we seem to be making moral evaluations and decisions, "good" means something akin to excellence. The fact that we treat goodness like a property indicates that it's something possessed objectively, not just in virtue of our evaluations or attributions. Further, goodness in these contexts is something properly valued and admired, but not just due to ideals held by people or communities. What's good is properly admired in virtue of its excellence. Finally, excellence is something to which we aspire, which we pursue in the course of our lives. Whatever has the property of goodness will be the something that satisfies this pursuit (ibid.: 22).

Grant that we can analyze goodness as excellence. Assuming the standard Anselmian conception of God as unsurpassably excellent, if God exists, then God will be unsurpassably good. What implications does this have for the account of the ordinary property of goodness?

According to the Argument from Goodness, it indicates that the property best suited to play the roles of goodness is Godlikeness. First, many things that are excellent, like beautiful flowers, don't have attitudes, and so aren't capable of allegiance but are capable of resemblance. Second, Godlikeness is a property that points beyond us; but goodness, too, seems to point to something transcendent. Third, we would expect the property goodness to bear an asymmetrical relation to the supreme good. Godlikeness is asymmetric in the right way, for while good things resemble the supreme good – God – in limited respects, it's misleading to say that God resembles good things because God's nature and existence would be prior. Lastly, when we make judgments about goodness, we display confidence in applying the concept and some uncertainty about the underlying reality to which we refer. We also demonstrate confidence in our ability to determine what is Godlike, but if God is ineffable, then there remains much we don't know about the underlying reality to which resemblance to God points. Together, these points make a cumulative case for treating goodness as Godlikeness.

2.3.1 The Metaethical Anselmian Argument

The argument above doesn't entail the strong metaphysical thesis because God could fail to exist, and the concept of God could still serve as a standard or ideal, resemblance to which constitutes the property goodness. To secure God's role in the complete metaphysical explanation of goodness requires an additional argument.

Adams's Metaethical Anselmian Argument aims to show that if anything fulfills the role of supreme goodness, it must be God.

(1) Something with the property of being supremely good is either impossible, possible, or actual.
(2) Mere possibilities are objects of understanding.
(3) If there is a possible object with the property of being supremely good, there must be someone that understands it.
(4) However, humans can't understand supreme goodness. Only God could understand supreme goodness.
(5) Either being supremely good is impossible, or it is possible and an object of God's understanding, or actual.
(6) If it is possible, God must exist, so as to understand it.
(7) If God exists, then we already have a suitable candidate for something that actually instantiates the property of being supremely good (ibid.: 42–46).

The Metaethical Anselmian Argument secures a position for God in the metaphysical explanation of goodness.

2.3.2 Objections from Atheism and Apophaticism

An atheist could resist the Argument from Goodness in at least two ways. First, she might deny the conception of God Adams assumes, according to which necessarily, if God exists, God possesses the property of being supremely good. She might say instead that God is omnipotent and omniscient, but that we don't have sufficient reason to think God is excellent in an unqualified way because of some logical incompatibility of these perfections with excellences like omnibenevolence (Jonas, 1987: 9). This may amount to a rejection of the conception of God as the Anselmian being.

Second, the atheist can object that goodness as excellence does point to anything transcendent; this-worldly beings, she might say, display their own sort of mundane goodness that neither points to nor reduces to otherworldly goodness. The atheist would bear the burden of proof in blocking the relation to otherworldly goodness, since many religious traditions have well-developed accounts of goodness in the mundane as a sign of God's immanence. How effective this objection is depends on the theist's picture of how God's goodness relates to created goodness, and this will vary between versions of theism.

Some theists will have an axe to grind with the Argument from Goodness because it rests on a starting point they reject, even though they endorse the Anselmian conception of God. On some apophatic theisms, which emphasize

God's hiddenness and our inability to know and speak truly of God, it is inappropriate to think of God as goodness in any real, ontological sense. According to one interpretation of Pseudo-Dionysius, our knowledge of God always comes through symbols and signification, but there is a radical ontological gap between creation and God. Because of God's dissimilarity to us, we are stuck with symbols and "the sign never reaching its ground" (Fisher, 2001: 532). Pseudo-Dionysius goes so far as to say, "And the fact that the transcendent Godhead is one and triune must not be understood in any of our typical senses … nothing that is or is known can proclaim that hiddenness beyond every mind and reason of the transcendent Godhead which transcends every being. *We cannot even call it by the name of goodness*" (ibid.: 534, emphasis mine). Apophatic theists who endorse this claim will reject the claims that goodness is Godlikeness, if ordinary things and human beings can have that property, and that God has the familiar property of goodness to an unsurpassable degree.

2.3.3 Postmodern Theism's Objection to Ontotheology

Theists who adhere to a wide variety of postmodern theologies will have reason to reject the talk of God as a ground of morality, generally. Despite differences between the particular postmodern theologies, they all call into question "the onto-theological framework" on which there is a purely objective metaphysical reality, or fabric of the universe, of which God is author and object (Simmons, 2011: 174). The postmodern theologian worries that speaking this way objectionably domesticates God. We do better to think of God in a practical mode and in relation to us, as transcendent, loving, creative (Westphal, 2001).

The second issue such postmodern theists will take with metaphysical talk of God and morality has to do with the recognition that we occupy a particular vantage point in history and culture, and the place of God in our language and practices is dependent on that vantage point. When we understand what Vattimo calls the "experience of cultural pluralism" and "the historicity and contingency of existing," we will be moved to think of goodness not as an analysis of divine nature but as self-giving, hospitality, receptivity to others (ibid.: 179). Whatever relationship obtains between God and morality on these theistic views is not aptly captured by metaphysical analysis but in practical understanding.

2.4 The Explainer-Driven Argument

Data-driven arguments fall prey to objections whenever there is an alternative explanation in the neighborhood that seems to fare as well as the theistic one;

subjectivism, the moral fixed points view, or constructivism, for example. Mark Murphy proposes that theists can establish God's role in metaphysical explanations of morality through an explainer-driven argument (Murphy, 2011). The general form of the argument is this:

(1) Some moral phenomenon M obtains.
(2) It is part of God's essence that, if God exists, then God grounds moral phenomenon M.
(3) God exists.
(4) Therefore, God grounds M.

We can see the advantage of this approach straightway – it requires no comparison with other candidate explanations for the moral phenomenon. What matters here, though, is that the God be the sort of being that must ground M and thus explain the data in (1).

Since the only version of this argument articulated in the contemporary literature is Murphy's, we'll take it as our paradigm for the explainer-driven argument.

2.4.1 God and Moral Laws

First, consider the relationship between moral facts but moral laws. Moral facts are "first order facts involving act-types' moral necessity," like the fact that one ought not steal a person's organs (ibid.: 47). While laws of nature impose physical necessitation – for instance, when the property being negatively charged makes it the case that an electron repels positive charges – moral laws impose moral necessitation, for instance, when the property of being my organ makes it the case that one ought not steal it. Moral laws ground moral facts by making some properties select for certain act-types. This gives rise to premise (1):

(1) Moral laws obtain.

Next, suppose God has the perfection of sovereignty. God's sovereignty consists in God's being a source of all that is, and in having immediate control of all that is. One reason for thinking God has immediate, rather than mediated, control is that if God were to bring something into existence, that creature couldn't persist if God (per impossible) ceased to exist (ibid.: 65). This indicates that God's control is not mediated. Another reason is that God is supposed to be omnipresent as a sustainer of all the goings-on in the universe (ibid.: 67).

Given this conception of God's sovereignty, it follows that in a universe where there existed something whose source wasn't God and which wasn't in

God's immediate control, God could not exist. So if God does exist, nothing can fall outside the scope of God's control and sourcehood (ibid.: 67). This is just to say that God is essentially such that God necessarily grounds the existence of anything that exists and immediately controls it:

(2) It is part of God's essence that, if God exists, God necessarily grounds the moral laws by being their source and in immediate control of them.

As this is a necessary property of God, and

(3) God exists.

We can conclude the strong metaphysical thesis:

(4) God necessarily grounds moral laws.

2.4.2 Natural Law and Indifferent Deism

Murphy's argument hinges on what he takes to be a standard conception of divine sovereignty, drawing on prominent figures from the Christian tradition such as Aquinas and Suarez (ibid.: 67, n. 10). As becomes clear later, this account of sovereignty alienates many natural law theists. For by their lights, creaturely natures fully explain the norms that govern each kind of creature and select certain act types as normatively necessary for their flourishing. When it comes to rational creatures like us, our natures and reason together are supposed to be sufficient to ground the facts about what we ought and ought not do (e.g., Lisska, 1996). God's role in metaphysically grounding moral facts is in the causal history of the natures that ground those facts. As God chose to bring those natures into being, on the causal view of metaphysical explanation, this suffices for God's being part of the metaphysical explanation of moral facts.

Such control is too remote to meet the immediacy requirement on divine sovereignty according to Murphy. In fact, if human nature can provide us with an account of the activities and things that perfect a human life, then what explanatory role over and above being part of the causal history is left for God? None, Murphy argues. Once the natures exist, then God no longer needs to exist to sustain the moral norms they ground. But then, at a certain time, there is something that exists of which God need not be the source or in control, which violates the requirement for divine sovereignty.

The compatibility of natural law theory with God's being an essential explainer of moral laws seems also to depend on how we think of God's relation to time. Neither Murphy nor the natural law theorist he targets makes any explicit remarks about this, but suppose the natural law theorist is an *eternalist* – thinks that God is atemporal and always outside of time. Murphy's argument for the immediacy requirement won't work. Either God causes the natures' existence timelessly, where this is sufficient for sustaining them, or God does not. The (counterpossible) scenario where God ceases to exist and the natures persist in grounding their own norms takes for granted that there is a time at which the natures exist and God does not, as though God is *sempiternal* – in time (Padgett, 1992, see also Deng, 2018).

3 God and Moral Epistemology

Let's pivot now to questions about God and moral epistemology. Moral episte-mology encompasses theories of what moral truths we plausibly know and how we come to know them, arguments about the epistemic justification (or lack thereof) of our beliefs about moral and metaethical theories. In the first two subsections we'll consider what difference theism is supposed to make to how much of the moral truth we know and how we know it. Then we'll consider an epistemic objection to grounding morality in theism. Throughout, we see that theistic and antitheistic arguments presuppose certain contestable conceptions of God that fly under the radar.

3.1 Theism and Moral Skepticism

Skeptical theism is a view about the scope of our moral knowledge given a thin traditional theism. Atheists proposed the core idea of skeptical theism as a potential response to the evidential problem of evil (E-PoE). Further refinements of the argument made the initial skeptical theist proposal seem inadequate (Draper, 1996). Theists since then have developed more sophisti-cated arguments to show that it *can* defeat the best versions of the E-PoE (Bergmann, 2001, Rea, 2013).

The way skeptical theism blocks a key inference of the Evidential Argument from Evil is by forwarding a skeptical account of our moral knowledge as applied to divine action. Once this skepticism is inserted into the debate, the question is whether the theists can stop the skeptical bleeding – that is, whether it entails that we have too little moral knowledge. We'll review the evidential argument for the E-PoE to which skeptical theism responds, the skeptical theist strategy, worries about introducing too much skepticism to save theism, and the question of what a theist needs to claim about God to use the skeptical theist's strategy.

3.1.1 The Evidential Problem of Evil

Early versions of the argument from evil introduced the so-called logical problem of evil. If God exists, God is omnipotent, omniscient, and omnibenevolent (omniGod thesis). An omnibenevolent God wouldn't willingly allow certain evils to occur, and if that God were all powerful and could foresee evils' occurrence, God would stop them from occurring. The existence of God is logically incompatible with the occurrence of evils. Such evils do occur. Thus God doesn't exist (Mackie, 1955).

Most philosophers now admit that the logical PoE is too ambitious. All that's needed to overcome the argument is a defense: an account of possible justifying reasons for God permitting the evils we see. For then we can see that it is not impossible for the God of omniGod theism to exist and evils we know of to occur (e.g., Plantinga 1965). The logical PoE also must assume we have *complete modal* moral knowledge – of all the possible goods and evils that figure in an evaluation of permitting evils. Hence it has largely fallen out of favor.

The Evidential Argument from Evil enjoys the lion's share of the discussion:

(1) Some horrendous instances of evil occur in our world.
(2) We cannot identify any good that morally justifies an omniscient and omnipotent being permitting their occurrence.
(3) So probably, there is no good that would morally justify an omnipotent and omniscient being permitting their occurrence. (2)
(4) If God exists, God is omnipotent, omniscient, and morally perfect. (omniGod thesis)
(5) A morally perfect being doesn't permit evil it knows of and can prevent without moral justification.
(6) So if God exists, God doesn't permit evils without moral justification. (4, 5)
(7) Suppose God exists.
(8) So if there is no good that morally justifies an omniscient and omnipotent being permitting horrendous evils, those evils do not occur. (6, 7)
(9) But probably, there is no good that morally justifies an omniscient and omnipotent being permitting horrendous evils, and they do occur. (1, 3)
(10) Therefore probably, God does not exist (Rowe, 1996). (7, 8, 9)

This argument requires much less in the way of moral knowledge than deductive arguments from evil. All we need is *probabilistic* moral knowledge – that it's unlikely that there is some good that morally justifies God in permitting horrendous evils that occur. The argument infers what probably is the case, morally speaking (3), from the goods and evils we know of (2).

Suppose Romina witnesses a horrendous evil – she is at a party and walks in on several drunken men sexually assaulting a young woman, Christina. She asks herself whether a totally powerful and knowledgeable God would have moral reason to permit this. *I can't think of any good that would justify God in standing by and letting this happen*, she thinks. *If God does exist, then God wouldn't let this happen unless there were some good moral justification for it.* We would certainly understand if Romina doubts God's existence after this episode. What makes sense of it is the assumption that Romina hasn't missed any significant possible goods that would morally justify God's permitting the assault.

3.1.2 Skeptical Theism

Skeptical theism blocks this inference from (2) to (3) with an alternative moral epistemology. The theism of skeptical theism is defined by the omniGod thesis (Bergmann, 2001: 279). The moral skepticism involves the endorsement of three claims:

ST1: We have no good reason for thinking that the possible goods we know of are representative of the possible goods there are.

ST2: We have no good reason for thinking that the possible evils we know of are representative of the possible evils there are.

ST3: We have no good reason for thinking that the entailment relations we know of between possible goods and the permission of possible evils are representative of the entailment relations there are between possible goods and the permission of possible evils (Bergmann, 2001).

If Romina were to accept ST1-3, she might think: *What happened to Christina seems unredeemable to me, but I know very little about possible moral justifications; possibly, there are goods for Christina that I can't begin to imagine, and God's permitting this assault is necessary to Christina's experiencing those goods.* Romina can accept that what happened is a horrendous evil (1) and that no good she knows of would justify God's permitting it (2). But her uncertainty about her grasp of possible goods and evils keeps her from inferring (3) that probably there is no good that would morally justify God's permitting Christina's assault.

So far, so good. But look at things from Christina's perspective. She might expect that if God exists and allows her to suffer a horrendous evil for the sake of a good, God will offer her assurance or comfort. When God is silent, this raises her doubts. Rowe calls this the Argument from Divine Silence:

(1) When God permits a horrendous evil for a good beyond our epistemic ken, God will not be silent but will make every effort to be consciously present to us during our period of suffering, explain why he is permitting us to suffer, and give special assurances.

(2) Many humans suffer horrendous evils and experience divine silence.

(3) So it is not the case that God permits a horrendous evil for a good beyond
our epistemic ken. (Rowe, 1996)

Skeptical theism can address the problem that arises from Christina's perspective, too. If ST1 and ST2 are true, we have reason to reject (1) because it assumes that a certain good – divine comfort – can temporarily ameliorate the evil of suffering, and that it's so good that God obviously has a requiring moral reason to give comfort to sufferers of evil. Skeptical theism says we're not positioned to know that. There could be further goods we don't know of that justify the divine silence following evil. We can't infer that probably there is no good that justifies the divine silence (Bergmann, 2001: 283).

3.1.3 The Too-Much-Skepticism Objection

This defense of theism against the E-PoE seems to entail an unpalatable moral epistemology. We don't want skeptical theism to commit us to *too much* moral skepticism. That would be dialectically unsatisfying, hiking up the price of rescuing theism from the E-PoE. Let's sharpen up the picture of how skeptical about moral knowledge the skeptical theist must be, then.

The skeptical theist asserts that the skepticism she means to endorse is

> extremely modest and completely appropriate, even for those who are agnostic about the existence of God. It is just the honest recognition of the fact that it wouldn't be the least bit surprising if reality far outstripped our understanding of it. (ibid.: 284)

One need only be skeptical of the claim that there's no moral justification for *God* to permit the evils we see occurring. In fact, skeptical theists sometimes present the challenge of the evidential problem in terms of "potentially *God-justifying* reason for permitting some horrific evil" (Bergmann and Rea, 2005, my emphasis).

Additionally, it's possible that we could come to know, of a particular evil, that there's no God-justifying reason for permitting it by other means than induction. I could have knowledge via moral intuition that the annihilation of infant souls is not the kind of evil any good could justify allowing, and infer that the goods and evils I know of are sufficient to judge this case. But my knowledge that there's no God-justifying reason for permitting infant annihilation isn't based on induction from goods and evils I know about (Bergmann, 2014: 212). Further, ST1-3 are claims about goods and evils, not deontic principles. We could know deontological moral principles like, "Never intend an evil that good may result," and that these principles constrain divine action as well as human action (Bergmann, 2012: 29). It could be that our moral knowledge regarding human actions is capacious, divine action, meager.

Can the skeptical theist circumscribe her skepticism in this way without incoherence or being ad hoc (Trakakis and Nagasawa, 2004; Almeida and Oppy, 2003)? The main concern is that skeptical theism's skepticism creeps into the domain where we think we have, and need, robust knowledge: morality that applies to ordinary human actions and attitudes. Call this the Too-Much-Skepticism objection (Rea, 2013: 486). The Too-Much-Skepticism objection could show that theism has negative implications for moral epistemology if skeptical theism is the best defense against the E-PoE.

On one version of the objection, skeptical theism requires us to mistrust the moral appearances, even when it comes to states of affairs and actions that we don't think of as beyond our epistemic ken (Jordan, 2006). Take an ordinary event like shopping at the grocery store, for example. ST2 indicates that, while grocery shopping for my family might seem to me a morally neutral or even good activity, for all I know there is a possible evil I perpetrate in grocery shopping. Possible evils need not resemble or be easily inferred from evils I know of, so for all I know, there is a great evil involved in my going grocery shopping that outweighs any good my shopping might do. If something as apparently innocuous as grocery shopping can be or cause evil unbeknownst to us on skeptical theism, then the view implies we don't have much safe moral knowledge.

Another version of the objection concerns its practical implications. A small child drowning in a pond looks like a thoroughly evil state of affairs worth preventing. Yet granting ST1-3, for all we know, there's a great good that justifies God's letting the child drown. (Maybe the child will be the youngest saint and receive a place of great honor in heaven forever.) Recognizing this may generate hesitation to save the child from drowning, lest we undermine the great good God intends to bring about in permitting this (Almeida et al., 2003: 505–6).

(1) We (human beings) are always (at least) morally permitted not to interfere with the purposes of God.
(2) For all we can tell, there are divine purposes in allowing certain evils.
(3) Therefore, for all we know, we are morally permitted not to interfere with those evils.

On skeptical theism, willingly allowing a child to drown is permissible. It's not just that any view that yields this result is deeply flawed, but that such a view could have wide-ranging and potentially detrimental practical effects.

In general, we think of correct moral judgments and decisions as requiring an all-things-considered perspective, taking into account all the relevant goods, evils, and entailment relations between them. When asking whether it's morally permissible for a physician to perform surgery on a pregnant woman that will end the life of the fetus, we consider a host of possible goods, evils, and relations between them (whether the bad of the fetus dying can be outweighed by the good of saving the mother's life, for instance). Without some reasonable confidence in our ability to discern the considerations that deserve to be weighed, we face the possibility of decisional paralysis. As one critic says, "If we should be skeptical about the reliability of our all-things-considered value judgments, then we are morally paralyzed" (Rutledge, 2017: 269). Does skeptical theism commit the theist to paralyzing and wide-ranging moral skepticism?

Maybe not. Facts about goods and evils are one thing, facts about right and wrong actions are another. Rightness facts are mediated by moral knowledge: a person does something right or wrong only relative to the goods and evils she knows of. Or, perhaps there is a deontological principle M* that confers rightness on action based on what the agent knows. M* could direct an omniscient God to act very differently from us, and still be a general moral principle governing divine and human action.

Another reply would appeal to the familiar idea in literature on moral reasons that plausibly, there is some accessibility relation that must obtain between a person and a moral reason for that person to be held responsible for her action or called morally irrational for her action. The skeptical theist could endorse a factoring account of reasons where what reasons there are is a separate question from what reasons a person has; a person has a reason to perform an action only when the reason is epistemically accessible to her, and a person's rationality should be assessed on the basis of the reasons she has (Lord, 2018). Thus, if there are reasons against attempting to curb Christina's suffering completely based on goods outside Romina's epistemic ken, as in ST1-3, these have no bearing on what Romina *has* moral reason to do.

A skeptical theist can also circumscribe her skepticism by adopting a popular view of blameworthiness on which a person is blameworthy only if she meets certain knowledge conditions. Ignorance of goods, evils, and entailment relations between them is grounds for excuse, as long as that ignorance isn't itself blameworthy (Rosen, 2003). By making use of extant theories of reasons, rationality, and blame that relativize moral evaluations of actions to the agent's knowledge, skeptical theists can ensure that her moral skepticism doesn't creep into evaluations of human actions while still applying to divine actions (including omissions).

Taking stock, how much moral skepticism is entailed by skeptical theism? If theism is true, on this view, we should be skeptical that our judgments about the goodness and badness of states of affairs and objects are reliable. When it comes to actions, the story depends on the independent metaethical account of right action, moral reasons or obligations, or blameworthiness the skeptical theist endorses.

On the one hand, whether an action is right or wrong may just depend on whether the state of affairs it constitutes or produces is good or bad. Similarly with whether an agent performing it is praiseworthy or blameworthy, whether we have moral reason to do it or refrain. If that sort of objectivist view is correct, then skeptical theism also entails that our moral evaluations of actions aren't very reliable.

On the other hand, whether an action is right or wrong may be a function of the goodness or badness of states of affairs and objects plus some accessibility condition – what facts about goodness and badness we know. If a moral action is wrong only if the person performing it has knowledge of the bads constituted and produced by it, then the skepticism of skeptical theism doesn't carry over to action. That is, as long as we know what goods and bads an agent is aware of, we can determine with a fair amount of accuracy which actions are right for her to perform.

3.1.4 The Divine Revelation Solution

Suppose we grant that theism entails skepticism only about possible goods and evils and entailment relations between them, *not* about our moral reasons, right actions, and apt blame. Some will find this dose of moral skepticism still too worrying. I want to diagnose this residual unease and suggest that a satisfying reply requires going well beyond thin traditional theism.

Here's the problem: it's unsettling to think that we are walking around, making moral judgments and acting on them, while totally unaware of many goods and evils that make a difference to which actions are objectively best. This is true even if we're not technically on the hook for the subpar actions we perform out of such ignorance. The skeptical theist's story about why we're not culpable for perpetuating evils we don't know of simply doesn't address *this* problem.

Put another way, if skeptical theism is true, then more informed and rational agents would be under radically different moral requirements than we are under. For our ignorance excuses us from meeting those requirements. But most of us, when we try to act morally, aren't just trying to act excusably. We're trying to act and live *well*. We want to respond appropriately to the moral goods there are. This orientation to the actual good drives moral inquiry. Skeptical theism tells us that if theism is true, our aspiring to discern moral truths is somewhat in vain. As long as skeptical theism provides resistence to the E-PoE, it simultaneously fuels the idea that reflection and philosophical investigation can't be sufficient to infer, from goods and evils we know of, probabilistic claims about goods and evils there are.

Theists can reply to this objection if they take on additional commitments about God. First, they can assert that God truthfully reveals God's reasons for acting through some body of Scripture or other form of divine revelation (perhaps religious experience). Next, revelation gives us a way of knowing God's reasons for acting on particular occasions (Rea, 2013: 485, 495). The believer's understanding of goods and evils is partly informed by divine revelation; if God chooses to reveal divine purposes that take into account goods and evils we otherwise wouldn't know of, then divine revelation can expand a believer's knowledge of possible goods and evils considerably. Moreover, if God takes into account all possible goods and evils when issuing divine commands, then these commands can act as heuristic devices, allowing those who obey them to better conform to the goods and evils that matter for living well. Finally, the religious tradition that safeguards that revelation can help the believer interpret Scriptures or religious experiences appropriately (e.g., Stump, 2010: 179–197). Therefore, on varieties of theism where divine revelation provides this knowledge or moral heuristic, people need not worry that they have too narrow a vision of what matters to act and live well. For we have noninductive methods of obtaining this moral knowledge.

Of course, a theist who denies the authority of Scripture or lacks established principles for supporting particular interpretations of Scripture won't be able to make this appeal. For if she doesn't have antecedent reasons to affirm Scripture, then the fact that Scripture lines up with moral appearances won't provide much evidence for its veridicality if skeptical theism's skepticism unsettles faith in our moral perception. Neither will a theist whose principle for interpreting revelation allows the individual to judge for herself whether divine commands apply to her, or whether Scripture is to be believed. The most plausible reply to the Too-Much-Skepticism objection requires a view of God much thicker than the omniGod thesis used in the E-PoE and skeptical theist's reply.

3.1.5 Which Theists Can Be Skeptical Theists?

Not all traditional theists can be skeptical theists. But not all theists need to be. In closing, let's identify the varieties of theism in which skeptical theism finds a natural home, those hostile to skeptical theism, and how a different sort of thick theism can reply to the E-PoE without introducing widespread moral skepticism.

The skeptical theist epistemology is at home on theisms on which God is so different from humans that we are quite limited in what we can say and know about God. This gives us reason to think we don't know much about the goods and evils that are relevant to the standard of action God must live up to, even if we know plenty about the human standard of action. Suppose God is all-loving, but God's love can't be described as equivalent to ideal human love. Whatever we know about love from the human case doesn't enable us to infer what God's love must be like (Rea, 2018: 63–89). Consequently, it makes sense to think of there being goods and evils and connections between them of which we know virtually nothing, but which don't bear on human ideals like perfect human love. Some apophatic theists say God is neither loving nor nonloving, but ineffable and transcendent. If it is a category mistake to speak of God as loving in a way analogous or similar to human love, then a claim that God is morally perfect or perfectly loving must be understood as nonfundamental, and not joint-carving (Jacobs, 2015).

Certain Islamic traditions have a conception of divine love that also suits skeptical theism. Al-Farabi and Avicenna imply that divine love doesn't involve personal relationship but "is the source and end of all creaturely goods and perfections, a love that is expressed most fully in God's providential care for us" (Stump and Green, 2015: 166). God cares providentially for humans by being the cause of their ultimate perfection. But for all we know, there are goods we don't know of that will enable us to achieve perfection. These goods could justify God's arranging the world in such a way that certain evils occur during our earthly lives. The *falsafa* tradition explicitly holds that humans obtain perfection in the afterlife. It consists in the understanding of God as first cause of being. On this account, a lack of moral knowledge in earthly life doesn't make a difference to whether one achieves human perfection. Providential care on the *falsafa* view, then, seems consistent with skeptical theism.

Theists disagree about what God's love implies about God revealing Godself to humans. Some traditional theists think of omnibenevolence as obviously entailing that God is known and knows humans personally. Some theists (and atheists) argue that being perfectly loving is not even conceptually compatible with either remaining hidden in the face of horrendous evils or failing to disclose relevant information about goods and evils or justifications for divine permission of horrendous evils to humans. This seems to be the underlying assumption in the Argument from Divine Silence. For those who think of perfect love this way, skeptical theism is a nonstarter (Schellenberg, 2015).

Here's the argument: First, God is whatever being is worthy of worship. Love is a divine attribute. Worship-worthy love must involve some self-revelation to the beloved. So God will reveal Godself to nonresistant nonbelievers and believers whom God loves. But nonresistant nonbelievers and others whom

God would love do not experience God revealing Godself to them. Apply this to Christina's case. If God exists, she can expect a revelation from God after her traumatic experience. Both she and Romina can know this, since it's a conceptual truth that God is loving in a way that is self-revealing. But the skeptical theist said we *can't* know this so-called conceptual truth: we can't know that there isn't some great good that justifies God in not revealing Godself to Christina in the wake of her trauma. Skeptical theism is incompatible with this conception of omnibenevolence.

Christian theism that takes the incarnation and atonement literally offers a poignant response to the problem of divine silence. For even if God remains hidden to a person for a limited period of time, perhaps to deepen the loving relationship, God has suffered and died, and has announced that this is for our redemption and comfort. In the atonement God displays the sort of great good that could justify horrendous human suffering, namely, the salvation of human-kind and victory over death.

Other Christian philosophers argue that God's hiddenness won't endure for a person's entire life or without spiritual consent – the person's wishing that God's will be done – because divine presence is a necessary part of a loving relationship with God (Cockayne, 2018). On this view, God makes known to those suffering at least that some entailment relation obtains between the evils God permits them to suffer and great goods, or at the very least one particular good that the suffering enables God to bring about, namely closer union with God. This can be made compatible with skeptical theism as long as we say the moral knowledge of the God-justifying goods for which God permits particular evils comes about through perception, testimony, or revelation, not by induction from the other goods and evils and entailment relations we know of.

Note that if union with God is plausibly deepened through suffering certain evils, we can offer a distinct defense against the E-PoE without skeptical theism's ST1-3. That is, there is a good we know of that plausibly provides a God-justifying reason for God's permitting certain evils, contra the Evidential Argument's second premise.

Now consider a variety of traditional theism that can resist the E-PoE without inviting skeptical worries at all. The general move of the Thomistic views is to provide reason to deny that moral perfection is a divine perfection – that it is properly part of the concept of God. If God is not morally perfect, then the Evidential Argument from Evil can't get started. For premise (1) of that argument says that God would not allow evil unless there were a moral justification for God's doing so. The natural law move does leave us with some degree of moral skepticism when it comes to reasons that apply to God – they aren't moral reasons. Happily, though, this skepticism doesn't bleed into the account of our moral knowledge.

The most recent argument for the claim that God is not necessarily morally perfect goes like this: The Anselmian God is perfectly loving. The extent to which God is perfectly loving doesn't outstrip the extent to which God is perfectly practically rational. But perfect rationality doesn't give one requiring reasons to promote the wellbeing of all creatures. So if morality gives agents reasons to promote others' wellbeing, then morality goes beyond rationality in this respect. God's being omnibenevolent doesn't guarantee that God is morally perfect (Murphy, 2017). If correct, the Evidential Argument from evil can't get started.

Other contemporary defenders of Thomism maintain that God does not belong to a genus or category of being; God is being itself. But for a being to be a moral agent, it must belong to a genus – namely, those beings whose nature makes moral action and character essential to their flourishing, such as human beings. The Thomist takes it to be a category mistake to ascribe moral perfection to God, since this assumes God's actions and character can be evaluated according to a standard set by a specific kind of nature (Davies, 2006). Hence this view has an argument against the initial premise in the evidential argument from evil – that God is morally perfect – and doesn't need to commit to any sort of moral skepticism in order to defend belief in God.

3.2 Theistic Replies to Debunking Arguments

In contrast to skeptical theism, some philosophers argue that theism uniquely explains our *robust* moral knowledge in the face of a family of challenges known as evolutionary debunking arguments. In this section we'll consider those arguments, replies that deny or don't require theism, and theistic replies. We'll also ask what assumptions about God must be at work for theistic responses to be compelling.

3.2.1 Evolutionary Debunking Arguments

Evolutionary Debunking Arguments (EDAs) challenge the possibility of widespread moral knowledge if moral realism is true (Joyce, 2001, Street, 2006). The argument starts with an empirical premise and a statement of moral realism:

> **Influence:** Evolutionary forces influence the development of our cognitive faculties, including the faculties we use to form moral beliefs and judgments.

> **Realism:** "If moral realism is true, there are at least some evaluative facts or truths that hold independently of all our evaluative attitudes." (Street, 2006: 110)

Further, given Influence, what our cognitive faculties are poised to do depends on what is adaptive. Having the cognitive power to discern mind-independent biological truths is adaptive: humans who can't recognize that a tiger is a predator are less likely to survive than those who can. But there's no obvious adaptive advantage to being able to recognize a mind-independent moral truth like "justice demands equal treatment of people of different races." Therefore,

> **Coincidence:** It is "extremely unlikely" that by happy coincidence, some large portion of our evaluative judgments ended up true due to natural selection. (Street, 2006: 122)

If Realism is true, then we would only end up with mostly true moral judgments if by an extremely unlikely coincidence, evolutionary pressures resulted in a faculty that tracked those truths. The moral realist is left with what Sharon Street calls a "Darwinian Dilemma":

> **Darwinian Dilemma:** If Realism is true, then we must embrace a "scientifically untenable" view of our cognitive faculties as tracking mind-independent moral truths or embrace skepticism about our moral knowledge. (Lott, 2018: 75)

A flurry of responses to this EDA has prompted important revisions. One secular reply with this effect points out a tacit but controversial assumption and argues against it. The early EDA assumes there are just two ways for our cognitive capacities to track the mind-independent moral truth to produce moral knowledge: by accident or by natural selection making them that way. Some secular realists claim this is a false dichotomy. Cultural context and training can also shape our capacities such that we generally track truths that aren't adaptive to track (Fitzpatrick, 2015: 886–7). Imagine Sara grows up in a community with a longstanding tradition of teaching children advanced mathematics and moral principles. Admittedly, there's nothing adaptive about having the ability to find an integral or discern whether one should eat meat, but Sara's community values this knowledge and passes it down. This longstanding tradition could explain why adults in Sara's community have reliable ability to track the mind-independent truth.

Debunkers reply by making more precise what our moral beliefs must look like to count as moral knowledge, and showing that beliefs gained by cultural influence won't count. We tend to think of knowledge as stable, sensitive, and safe. Formally,

> **Sensitivity**: S's belief that p is sensitive if and only if, in nearby possible worlds where p is false, S does not belief that p. (Ichikawa, 2011)

If Sensitivity is right, Sara's case doesn't illustrate a third way for us to get moral knowledge. For in nearby possible worlds Sara's culture could have remained the same but the moral truths been entirely different. In that case, Sara's exercise of her cognitive capacities would have led her and her peers to make systematically incorrect moral judgments. Their beliefs lack the sensitivity to count as knowledge.

A more recent EDA makes the assumption about moral knowledge explicit:

(1) "Our moral faculty was naturally selected to produce adaptive moral beliefs, and not naturally selected to produce true moral beliefs.

(2) Therefore, it is false that: had the moral truths been different, and had we formed our moral beliefs using the same method we actually used, our moral beliefs would have been different.

(3) Therefore, our moral beliefs are not sensitive.

(4) Therefore, our moral beliefs do not count as knowledge" (Bogardus, 2016: 640).

3.2.2 Failures of Secular Replies

A driving force behind theistic replies to EDAs is the apparent failure of secular realist replies. So, it's worth reviewing the best secular replies and objections to them to appreciate the motivation for theistic alternatives.

The most ubiquitous class of secular realist responses to EDAs is the minimalist response. Minimalists refrain from asserting any direct explanatory connection between moral truths and our moral beliefs. Instead, they posit a modal connection between moral truths and moral beliefs that gives our moral beliefs justification, even absent a direct explanatory connection (Korman and Locke, 2020).

A representative example of a minimalist response is the third-factor response. It aims to show that some factor besides the moral truth simultaneously explains our cognitive capacities' reliability in tracking moral truths and the obtaining of those moral truths. For instance, suppose it's a moral truth that humans have moral rights. Pietro has a belief that we have rights. This belief isn't adaptive, but it's adaptive for Pietro to have higher-order cognitive capacities, for this enables communities of people with this trait to survive disasters and recover from devastation more quickly. One reason is that such people tend to put effort into building technologies with long-term payoff, even if there is not short-term gain. Pietro's higher-order capacities – what enables him to understand and be motivated by the long-term/short-term tradeoffs – also dispose him to grasp the complex concept of a moral right (Wielenberg, 2010: 441–64). While the moral truth about rights doesn't directly explain Pietro's beliefs about rights, we can explain why evolution would select for the capacities that would produce those true beliefs.

Third-factor accounts like this, while innovative and clever, have to assume a moral truth *that is under dispute* to get going. We must assume, in the example above, that there *are* moral rights, so Pietro's moral beliefs are correct. (Sometimes debunkers complain that this amounts to question begging, but this isn't quite right; realists are allowed to make use of some claims entailed by the truth of their view, just not the truth of their view, absent defeaters.) Remember, debunkers object that the realist has to rely on a scientifically implausible coincidence to be sure of the truth about moral rights. On this third-factor account, Pietro's moral belief is formed by a faculty whose reliability in the moral domain is a coincidence. Luckily, the faculty that produces adaptive advantages also tracks the moral truth. The secular realist offers no further explanation for the third factor's having both properties of being adaptive and being good. So the third-factor accounts leave us with an unexplained coincidence (Morton, ms: 3).

The bigger obstacle for minimalist replies to overcome is an epistemic problem, namely, that our moral beliefs should be unaffected by our denying a direct connection between the moral truth and those beliefs. Korman and Locke offer the following analogy: Lois finds herself with an inescapable feeling that Goldbach's conjecture is necessarily true; then she remembers she's been hypnotized by watching a video. She decides to suspend her belief about Goldbach's conjecture – after all, perhaps it was suggested to her in the video, and the hypnotist got her to believe the conjecture not on the basis of anything that would make it true. Now she doesn't have any reason to think that something that makes Goldbach's conjecture true explains her intuitive belief. The rational thing to do in light of this is *suspend* her belief in the conjecture (Korman et al., 2020). The analogy teaches a lesson about explanatory connections and the rationality of belief. It isn't rational to retain a belief, B, when you lose a belief that whatever grounds the truth of B isn't explanatorily connected to your having B. Even if B is *in fact* safe or sensitive, by conceding that having B isn't explained by the truth of B, you violate a kind of internal rational requirement in holding onto B.

Applying this lesson to EDAs, the minimalist agrees to put to the side the claim that her moral beliefs are directly explained by whatever makes them true. Once she does this she gives up the game. For it's irrational to hold onto her moral beliefs in the course of the argument. She should suspend them, since she thinks they're explained by some non–truth-related factor (like the hypnosis in the Goldbach's example). Pietro continuing to believe that there are moral rights, while accepting that belief doesn't come about because it is true, doesn't make sense. Further, suppose Pietro learns his beliefs about rights are safe or sensitive. That would provide some evidence that there *is* an explanatory connection between his moral beliefs and the world. So it doesn't make sense to try to isolate the modal connection between beliefs and the facts as though it could exist with no explanatory connection (ibid.: 22–23).

3.2.3 Theistic Replies to Debunking

Traditional theism has resources to respond to EDAs that secular moral realists lack, according to atheists and theists in the debate. If they're right, theism provides a uniquely convincing defense of moral realism against evolutionary debunking arguments. Our present concern is whether that's true and whether its scope is appropriate, or only *some* theisms have this advantage.

The secular moral realist seems stuck with the assumption that our faculties track the moral truth reliably by massive coincidence or not sensitively enough to produce moral knowledge. But if God controls the ethical facts and causal order, then the charge of massive coincidence could be dropped (Bedke, 2009: 109). Thus, even atheists claim theism as the only hope for realists to respond to the debunking challenge:

> Things look different if we turn to God. Assuming God can know the truth in ethics, even if it is irreducible, he may create in us, or some of us, reliable dispositions. On this account, ethical principles *can* explain how we are disposed to form true beliefs [thus meeting the nonaccidental reliability constraint]. This is, I think, the only hope for ethical knowledge if the facts are constitutively independent of us. (Setiya, 2012: 114)

In these and similar passages, the line of reasoning seems to run:

(1) Grant Influence and Coincidence.
(2) On traditional theism, God directly creates or controls the development of human cognitive faculties.
(3) God knows or controls all the mind-independent moral truths.
(4) If traditional theism is true, then there is some further controlling causal influence ensuring human faculties track the mind-independent moral truth. (2, 3)
(5) If traditional theism is false, then Realism entails a scientifically implausible claim or we have no moral knowledge. (Darwinian Dilemma)
(6) Therefore, either traditional theism is false and moral realism entails moral skepticism, or traditional theism is true and we probably have moral knowledge.

Some theistic arguments to this effect lean on familiar reasoning from reformed epistemology to support (2). Here is the familiar line of thought: If God exists, we likely have certain truth-tracking cognitive faculties. When a belief is produced by the properly functioning cognitive faculties working according to a design plan successfully aimed at truth, that belief is warranted and thus counts as knowledge. Belief in God's existence is the result of properly functioning cognitive faculties working according to a divine design plan aimed at truth. Belief in God's existence is knowledge.

We can run a parallel argument by substituting "moral belief" for "theistic belief":

(1) "If God exists, then God created us in his image, loves us, desires that we know and love him, and is such that it is our end to know and love him."

(2) It is good for humans to have moral knowledge.

(3) "If God created us in his image, loves us, desires that we know and love him, and is such that it is our end to know and love him, then God is probably such that" God would create us with the ability to achieve what is good for us.

(4) So if God exists, then God probably created us in such a way that we would come to hold certain true moral beliefs.

(5) "If God probably created us in such a way that we would come to hold certain true [moral] beliefs, then [moral] beliefs are probably produced by cognitive faculties functioning properly according to a design plan successfully aimed at truth (and is thereby probably warranted)" (Moon, 2017; see Plantinga, 2011: chs. 3–4).

This argument is supposed to show that thin theism entails that we have robust moral knowledge.

Unfortunately, this particular argument fails for the very reason that third-factor accounts fail. It relies on a *substantive* moral premise *in the target range* of the evolutionary debunking argument: that a morally perfect being would ensure that humans have moral knowledge. In other words, while not all charges of question-begging stick to third-factor accounts, charges that one relies on a substantive premise under dispute are threatening, and this is precisely what the argument above does. The belief that moral perfection requires that particular divine action is a moral belief subject to evolutionary influence (Morton, ms).

The theist can revise the reply in three steps. First, she needs to distinguish the kind of moral knowledge EDAs target: substantive moral knowledge about what in particular is good or evil, right or wrong, independent of anyone's evaluative attitudes. Second, if a moral truth is mind dependent or not substantive, a moral realist is free to rely on it in her argument. Third, if the theist supposes God loves humans and God's reasons depend on that love, then any moral truths grounded by this theistic claim are mind dependent – they depend on God's evaluative attitudes. Now the theist can run this argument:

(1) God is rationally perfect, responding appropriately to the reasons there are.
(2) God loves human beings.
(3) Because of God's love of human beings, God has a mind-dependent reason to bring about our good.
(4) Our good requires our having moral knowledge.
(5) We have no reason to think there is a countervailing or undercutting reason for God to not bring about our moral knowledge.
(6) A perfectly rational being will act on the basis of the reasons there are in the absence of countervailing or undercutting considerations for that action.
(7) God acts on a reason God has to bring about our moral knowledge (Morton, ms: 17–18).

This revised argument makes no substantive assumptions about what is morally good or bad.

3.2.4 Thick Theisms and EDAs

The successful theistic reply to EDAs requires additional assumptions about what God is like and what we can know about God's attitudes.

First, the reply assumes that God asserts a fair amount of control over the development of human cognitive faculties and/or the moral facts. For God must be able to bring it about that humans have moral knowledge. And the argument from reformed epistemology gives an account of how this happens – God directly creates or indirectly controls the development of whatever cognitive faculty produces moral beliefs. Or, God might leave our faculties alone but control moral truths such that we reliably track them, whatever kind of faculties evolution produces. God's being the omniGod or creator doesn't entail that God actively or intentionally guides the evolutionary development of humans or controls the moral facts, however. This is a substantive assumption about divine action to be added to thin theism.

Second, the argument assumes God loves and as a result, desires to promote the good of all human beings in premises (2) and (3). This is critical because the reason to bring about our moral knowledge needs to depend on an evaluative attitude, in this case God's desire. For then no premise of the argument is a mind-independent moral truth of the sort the EDA calls into question. But we've already seen one way some theists resist this claim about God.

Remember Murphy's argument (subsection 3.1.5) that the Anselmian God doesn't have requiring reason to promote the wellbeing of creatures, only a requiring reason to not harm them.

Some skeptical theists might not endorse premise (3) or the conclusion of this theistic reply. The reply requires an inference from God's being loving to God bringing about our moral knowledge. But skeptical theism blocks the inference from the existence of an omnibenevolent God to knowing what, specifically, God intends:

> Alvin Plantinga assumes that if God exists it is obvious that our belief-forming faculties are reliable ... given our scepticism, we are not sanguine about [this] inference (God might well have other interests, motives, etc. than the few that we are able to decipher). (McBrayer and Swenson, 2012: 145)

Is God's desire for us to have moral knowledge, given its role in our wellbeing, one of the few divine motives we can decipher?

Suppose it is. Remember that skeptical theists are not committed to broad skepticism, but only to the view that in some cases we can't know what God would do (Moon, 2017). Since God is omniscient and omnipotent, we might derive general conclusions about God's intentions and actions from claims about God's knowledge. For instance, if E occurs and God knows that his actions would result in E, then God intended E (Moon, 2017). But this principle of inference can be cast into doubt by counterexamples.

> Suppose God intends to make a bush look like it is on fire. God might also know that this event will cause a nearby plant to cast a shadow. But the casting of the shadow might not have been God's intention ... God could have been completely indifferent to the shadow. (ibid.)

Maybe we can derive support for the claim that God intends and brings about our having moral knowledge via another inferential principle like

> If God has some desire for E to occur and God knew that his actions would result in E's occurring, then God intended for E to occur. (ibid.)

Unfortunately, this principle also faces a counterexample. Suppose God desires to be in relationship with Fred. Possibly, God also has a reason to not use this desire as God's reason for action. Perhaps God's directly pursuing Fred would be coercive and lead to a relationship in which Fred doesn't freely love God. God might then creatively will another action that has a happy byproduct: enabling Fred to be in relationship with God through Fred's free decision (ibid.). Here, knowing what God desires doesn't give us knowledge of what God intends, even if God is omniscient.

Thus, even granting that God desires human wellbeing (perhaps because of our conception of omnibenevolence), skeptical theists shouldn't grant the revised theistic reply to EDAs. The reply relies on an inference from (2) to (3) and (5). But for all we know, God might have a reason to not act on God's desire for our wellbeing by giving us moral knowledge. God might have reason to create a world where evolutionary influence distorts our cognitive faculties. Maybe such a world affords God more opportunities to forgive us and save us from graver evils and noetic effects of sin than in the world where our cognitive faculties produce moral knowledge.

There is a notable tension, then, between skeptical theism and theistic replies to general debunking arguments, even though both are supposed to operate on the same thin traditional theism. Andrew Moon (2017) suggests that what he calls the bare-theism-based argument given by Plantinga (and presumably our version of it applied to moral beliefs) should be replaced by religion-based arguments. While Plantinga's argument "moves from the bare existence of God, to claims about God's intentions" the religion-based arguments proceed "from substantive claims about God's intentions already made or implied in an established religion" (ibid.). Religion-based arguments serve as a paradigmatic example of the kind of moves I've stressed we need to make in discussions of theism and morality more generally.

For example, a certain version of Christianity can offer the following theistic argument against the debunking challenge. First, "God loves humans, has special plans to redeem humans and bring about relationship with them, and intends for himself to be glorified among them" (Moon, 2017). Second, imagine that God expresses in Scriptures that God can't be in relationship with beings who are morally impure or bad according to their kind, and so God can't achieve God's stated purpose without humans being morally good. Add the plausible view that one can't be morally good without moral knowledge (that is, no one can be morally good by sheer accident or without acting based on knowledge). These substantive commitments about what God wants and intends allow the Christian to say that if God exists, our cognitive faculties reliably track mind-independent moral truths.

Another strand of Christian thought inspired by Aquinas circumvents the need for sensitive moral knowledge altogether. On this view, the noetic effects of sin are so drastic that there is no guarantee that we know what in particular is good or what God wants from us. Instead, we only know that whatever God wills, God wills it under the description "good" and whatever God nils, God nils under the description "evil." God extends grace to human beings by making friendship with God, rather than moral uprightness, the only condition for perfect happiness in the afterlife. And friendship with God, God determines, only requires that the human friend not intentionally set themselves against God's purposes – that is, will what they think God nils and nil what they think God wills (Jeffrey, 2015). So even when a human is mistaken about what in particular is good or bad, she can act in ways required for eventual perfect happiness by acting according to conscience (Jeffrey, forthcoming). For then she meets the condition for friendship with God.

We can draw two lessons from the discussion of moral epistemology in this and the previous section. One, thin theism by itself underdetermines one's moral epistemology. It doesn't guarantee that our moral knowledge is robust, nor does it guarantee it is incredibly limited. Two, we need to pay attention to particular thick theisms to draw conclusions. Not every variety of traditional theism affords a good reply to Evolutionary Debunking Arguments, but promising responses can be generated from within religious views that accept certain substantive claims about God's intentions and purposes.

3.3 The Naturalist Explanationist Argument

The final set of arguments in moral epistemology we'll consider target all versions of moral nonnaturalism, including theistic ones, as epistemically unjustified. The debate begins with a problem with belief in moral properties called Harman's Challenge. Below we'll look at Harman's Challenge, the naturalist realist response to it – the Explanationist Argument – and whether it creates an unsurmountable difficulty for accounts that ground moral properties in some theistic property.

3.3.1 Harman's Challenge and Naturalist Realism

Begin with Harman's Challenge:

(1) We only have reason to believe in real moral properties or facts if they are part of the best explanation of observable phenomena. (Enoch, 2007: 24)
(2) The best explanation of observable moral phenomena doesn't require the existence of real moral properties or facts. (ibid.)
(3) Therefore we don't have reason to believe in real moral properties or facts.

Two points about Harman's Challenge are worth noting. As Enoch explains, "What underlies the explanatory requirement is, after all, a highly plausible methodological principle of parsimony. Kinds of entities should not be unnecessarily multiplied, redundancy should be avoided" (ibid.: 26). Further, the kind of explanation at issue in the explanatory requirement is epistemic. It's about what we have reason to believe, not a metaphysical thesis about the nonexistence of moral properties. This means that Harman's Challenge leaves untouched the possibility that a theistic account of morality is true but not epistemically rational to believe.

Harman's Challenge puts pressure on moral realists to show that realist moral properties do play some important role in the best explanation of observable phenomena. Naturalist moral realists have responded by offering so-called Explanationist Arguments. While there are several versions in the literature, we'll focus on a recent formulation:

(1) "We have reason to believe that a property P is genuine if a predicate S figures ineliminably in a good explanation of observed phenomena and in that explanation S refers to P.

(2) Moral predicates feature ineliminably in good explanations of observed phenomena, and in those explanations they refer to moral properties.

(3) We have reason to believe that moral properties are genuine" (Sinclair, 2011: 15).

This argument tells us we may justifiably believe in moral properties because the terms we use to refer to them play an ineliminable role in the best explanation of observed moral phenomena.

Initially, there doesn't seem to be anything distinctively naturalist, or anti-supernaturalist, about the explanationist argument. Couldn't the theist run the very same argument for realism about moral properties and then add her theistic analysis of those properties? The data-driven arguments of sections 2.1–2.3 seem to do precisely this.

Naturalists claim that they have a leg up on nonnaturalist and supernaturalist accounts of moral properties. For Harman's Challenge implies we're licensed to believe in observable, empirically testable entities or unobserved entities with observable effects. Nonnatural properties, and certainly supernatural properties, are not observable or empirically testable; nor are they supposed to have empirically observable effects. By contrast, naturalist realism says that moral properties reduce to natural properties (like being conducive to survival or to group fitness). The property of being just is whatever natural properties constitute it. And when we use the moral predicate "just," we refer to that or those natural properties. But natural properties are per hypothesis empirically testable or have observable effects, given some theory that explains their causal role in bringing about what we observe.

Here is an analogy. We are perfectly epistemically justified in believing in muons, though we can't observe them, because we can empirically verify their effects and our physical theory works out the causal connection between muons and observed phenomena. Similarly, we are perfectly epistemically justified in believing in natural properties like goodness or justice that have causal effects that can be empirically tested.

3.3.2 Varieties of Theism and Supernaturalist Realism

A theist who grounds moral properties in supernatural properties supposedly cannot comply with the rules set out by Harman's Challenge. The theist who says being morally obligatory reduces to being-commanded-by-God, for instance, insists that being commanded by God is the referent of whatever moral predicate figures in the best explanation of moral phenomena. But a property like being-commanded-by-God isn't empirically testable. And, the naturalist assumes, it won't have empirically testable effects either. So it fails to figure in the best explanation of the phenomena while meeting Harman's Challenge.

Generating a reply on behalf of theistic views is not so easy. It may be that our *beliefs* in supernatural properties figure in the best explanation of moral phenomena. For example, perhaps our *belief* that moral obligations come from a divine lawgiver best explain the observed phenomena of our feeling bound by obligations or our predicate "morally obligatory" – this seemed to be Anscombe's point. But Harman's Challenge tells us that this isn't sufficient, for our supernatural beliefs might explain the moral phenomena, but this doesn't entail that the *real properties* our beliefs are *about* must exist for us to explain the moral phenomena. Our belief that moral obligations are divine commands could be systematically mistaken and still explain why we have the feeling that, say, moral obligations are binding or are second-personal.

Suppose the theist claims that the phenomenon of people's beliefs *that moral obligations are divine commands* is best explained by *the existence of supernatural properties* like "being commanded by God." Would this vindicate supernaturalist moral realism? This seems unlikely without a further story, or a theoretical view about justification like phenomenal conservatism on which seemings generate justification of belief. But the story or theory will need to be nuanced, for parallel moves look untenable: the widespread belief in witches in earlier centuries wasn't best explained by the existence of witches, nor does the best explanation for belief in Big Foot appeal to the existence of Big Foot.

An alternative, I suggest, is to hold a variety of thick theism on which God can be a cause of things in the natural order, including moral phenomena. For instance, suppose God is related to the natural order in the way suggested by some of the replies to evolutionary debunking arguments such as Morton's. On Morton's view, a result of having moral knowledge is that one has a higher chance of achieving human (nonmoral) wellbeing. Suppose we can observe and measure human (nonmoral) wellbeing, and several people have this wellbeing. Morton can argue that, since God creates our cognitive faculties and guides evolutionary processes such that they develop a capacity to reliably track moral truths, the existence of such a God is part of the best explanation for our having moral knowledge. But given that moral knowledge is a chief ingredient in human wellbeing, we need an explanation for how persons with observed high degrees of wellbeing have moral knowledge. So then, God will figure in the best explanation of the observed human wellbeing. All we need to do is add to thin traditional theism a story about God's involvement with the natural world such that God's involvement is the best explanation for some observed natural phenomenon, such as wellbeing.

4 God, Moral Attitudes, and Moral Motivation

In this final section, we swivel our attention to practical questions of interest in metaethics to see how theism may or may not affect our answers. We will consider whether certain practical stances, such as optimism, make more sense given theism than atheism, as well as whether theism provides a unique story about the rationality of moral motivation and moral action. Two of the prominent arguments in the literature here explicitly reference a thick version of theism. We'll consider which particular claims about God a theist has to buy for those arguments to work.

4.1 The Problem of Evil for Everyone

Typically we think of the problem of evil as a problem for *theistic belief.* But there is another recent version of the problem of evil that is quite different in that it is a problem for atheists and theists alike, and it is a problem for the practical attitude of optimism rather than for belief in God's existence or nonexistence. This version of the problem of evil is called the problem of systemic evil (PoSE) (Nagasawa, 2018). Yujin Nagasawa has argued that theists can overcome PoSE more easily than atheists. Let's look at this argument and consider how variations on theism or atheism might affect it.

4.1.1 The Problem of Systemic Evil

The problem of systemic evil refers to the fact that the biological system that produced us seems rife with horrible pain, suffering, and death. Consider some of the basic facts of our evolutionary history. Organisms compete for scarce resources, encounter brutal suffering and death, and the extinction of species after generations of individuals have vainly sacrificed to perpetuate their kind. For roughly four billion years a vast number of organisms have suffered and died at the hands of this biological system – "nature red in tooth and claw" (Tennyson, 1851). These cruel natural events are produced by a complex and methodical biological *system*. Human existence depends on the evolutionary processes of this system. We wouldn't be here at all if it weren't for the massive carnage of other organisms at the hand of natural selection (Nagasawa, 2018: 156).

At the same time, many people regularly express *existential optimism*. Existential optimism is a practical attitude or stance toward the world that treats the world as "overall a good place" and holds that "we should be grateful for our existence in it" (ibid.: 154). Even atheists quite vocal about the cruelty of our biological system defend this kind of optimism. Richard Dawkins, for instance, says, "When I lie on my back and look up at the Milky Way . . . when I look at the Grand Canyon . . . I'm overwhelmingly filled with a sense of, almost worship . . . it's a feeling of sort of an abstract gratitude that I am alive to appreciate these wonders" (ibid.: 162).

The PoSE is that this practical attitude doesn't make sense in light of the overwhelming evidence that our existence owes to the great suffering and death of countless other sentient organisms, human and nonhuman. If we currently have the correct account of the biological system that produced us, there is not a nearby possible world in which we exist but widespread misery, destruction, and death of other animals does not. So it's not as though we can separate our existence from the biological system that produced us and express gratitude for it while regretting the existence of the biological system; even though this is psychologically possible, it seems deeply irrational.

4.1.2 Theistic Advantage?

If atheism is true, then this material universe is all there is. Let's make the simplifying assumption that all the evaluative facts about the universe consist in facts about *sentient* creatures. Given evolutionary history, the majority of evaluative facts in this world are negative. There may be many positive facts due to human life, even positive to an intensely high degree. But it seems this world on the whole is more bad than good.

Atheism has no further resources to resist this characterization, since it denies the existence of any nonmaterial objects and the afterlife. So as long as existential optimism is an irrational practical attitude to hold on the supposition that the world is mostly bad, and we depend for our existence on it, atheism seems irreconcilable with existential optimism.

On the contrary, theism can dissolve this apparent conflict by undermining the appearance that the world is mostly bad. If theism is true, Nagasawa argues, then "there is an immaterial being that exists beyond our material universe, and that there is also an afterlife which is beyond our life in the material universe" (ibid.: 160). By adding the existence of an afterlife, the theist makes a soul-making theodicy available according to which creatures' pain and suffering are redeemed by the role they play in improving the souls of those creatures, such that they can enjoy perpetual paradise. Or, if an immaterial God exists, then skeptical theism might be true and probably the evaluative facts we know of aren't representative of the evaluative facts there are. Thus, we can refrain from believing that the world is mostly bad on the basis of empirical biological evidence, and maintain existential optimism. The conclusion of the argument, then, states that "the problem of systemic evil is primarily a problem of evil for atheists" (ibid.: 161).

4.1.3 Which Theism Has the Advantage over Which Atheism?

Adding God to one's ontology may seem to change the balance of positive and negative evaluative facts by itself. For if God is part of the universe and maximally evaluatively good, then God's existence supplies enough positive facts to outweigh all the negative facts about the observed biological system. Emanationist views of God seem especially well suited to give this sort of reply. The accounts of God on which God is wholly other and distinct from the universe, though, cannot use this particular strategy. For then facts about God are decidedly *not* facts about the value of the world.

For theists who deny that God is part of the universe, the reply will need to appeal to an afterlife. On a Christian view like that of Marilyn McCord Adams (2006, 2008), God uses the afterlife to defeat evils, eradicating them and redeeming them by bringing about great good for each individual who experienced evil. The redemptive aspect of this view, however, seems unique to Christianity and some varieties of Judaism, since standard Islamic pictures feature an afterlife where goods come about for individuals as rewards for their deeds. Further, the Adams-style strategy remains out of reach for orthodox Jewish annihilationists. They deny the existence of an afterlife, and instead see the redemption God brings about for God's people as occurring on earth through the reign of a Messiah. Even supposing that such a reign is quite lengthy in human time, it is hard to believe that it would eradicate the underlying biological systemic evils or that the positive effects of that reign could outnumber the negative ones over billions of years in earth's history.

Perhaps the best strategy for the latter kinds of theists, then, is to deny the aggregative evaluative assumption. The assumption is that we can arrive at a correct account of the world's value on the whole by aggregating values that

Here is the first part of the argument:

(1) "There are certain things that a person should not, under any circumstances, be willing to do." Call these *absolutely prohibited actions*.

(2) "There are outcomes that, given a choice, no decent person would allow." Call these *absolutely prohibited outcomes*.

(3) In some circumstances, the only way to avoid allowing an absolutely prohibited outcome is to perform an absolutely prohibited action.

(4) In some circumstances, the only way to avoid performing an absolutely prohibited action is to allow an absolutely prohibited outcome.

(5) Therefore, in some circumstances, one must do something (morally) prohibited. (Ebels-Duggan, 2015: 90–91).

Premise (5) tells us that someone may do everything in her power to live a good life and still find herself faced with the choice between doing something disgraceful or allowing something horrendous. And no one walks away from that kind of choice unmarred. This realization threatens serious despair:

(6) When moral agents discover there's no guarantee they won't find themselves in a dilemma of the kind described in (5), they will have reason to despair.

The practical problem isn't only about moral purity. We might also despair in light of (5) because we realize doing what's morally right could lead to unhappiness. Happiness consists in desire satisfaction. We might think a virtuous person could cultivate only morally pristine desires, such that doing the right thing will lead to her happiness. But even these desires, like a desire for one's child's wellbeing, leave one vulnerable to the problem in (5).

Consider the case of Wesley Autrey, who jumped in front of a subway in front of his children in order to save a stranger having a seizure on the tracks. Imagine that the world did not cooperate as well as it did (Autrey successfully saved the stranger and survived). Autrey clearly desires the wellbeing of his children. But doing his duty in helping the stronger could have come at the cost of his own happiness, not only because it frustrated a desire to live, but also because of the trauma and loss his children would have suffered after seeing their father die a horrific death. If there is no guaranteed reward of happiness for those who do what's morally right, let alone heroic, it would be reasonable to despair at the heavy burden of the moral law under which we have to labor.

4.2.2 The Need for Hope in God

To solve this problem, some suggest we need hope in God (Ebels-Duggan, 2015; Chignell, 2014). Interestingly, not just hope in any sort of God will do the work; the object of our hope must be the God emerging from the Christian religion.

A natural place to look for a remedy for despair is whatever supplies the contrary attitude, namely, hope. Hope and despair have the same object – a great good seen by the agent as difficult to obtain. Imagine that Andres and Brooke both strongly desire to get a college degree. Both are first-generation college students and have to work forty hours a week to pay for room and board, while taking a full course load to maintain their scholarships. One year in, Brooke sees the arduousness of attaining her goal and in despair, withdraws. Andres sees the same difficulty, but pursues his goal nonetheless, demonstrating hope. Hope and despair respond to the same object but in opposing manners. What we need to solve the practical problem of the right and the good is grounds for hope in some sort of coincidence of good outcomes (including our happiness) and good actions. Call this "the happy coincidence."

Why might secular attempts to supply hope in the happy coincidence fall short? For one, Ebels-Duggan explains, they will be hard-pressed to find empirical evidence on which to base such hope. Secular theories are beholden to empirical evidence in a way theistic theories aren't. A truly secular theory can't appeal to any otherworldly goods, agents, or states of affairs to explain or motivate hope in the happy coincidence. But all we need to do is look around to see that "acting well apparently does not reliably lead to good outcomes" (Ebels-Duggan, 2015:98).

Perhaps a secular theorist can attempt to show that hope can be gotten cheaper – all one needs is a belief that it's likely one will attain the great good one desires. One can get psychological hope that way, maybe, but it will be irrational. Suppose Brooke can muster up hope by forming the belief that the good she wants isn't so difficult for her to obtain, despite her lack of evidence for this, or that even though many people in her predicament don't finish their degrees she will be different. Analogously, the secular moral theory could try to coach agents into believing against the evidence that acting morally won't leave the world a worse place than one found it, and won't jeopardize one's own happiness, to shore up hope in the happy coincidence.

The obvious problem with this sort of method is that the resultant hope would be a kind of bad faith or *irrational* hope. That is, the cognitive basis of such hopes is irrational when it runs contrary to the person's evidence (Milona, 2018). The secular theorist needs to provide a *rational* basis for hope in the happy coincidence.

Return, then, to the hope based on empirical belief. We could say that hope in the happy coincidence is epistemically rational just in case it is epistemically rational to believe that the happy coincidence is merely *possible*, at least for some people. What's outlandish is hoping for what one believes to be impossible, or on the basis of a belief that the object of hope is possible when one's evidence supports the claim that it's *im*possible.

Grant to the secular theorist the epistemic rationality of believing the happy coincidence is *possible*, at least for some people. Now all the secular theory needs is a way of accounting for the practical rationality of hope in that outcome. Many accounts of hope have it that a hope for p is practically rational just in case it furthers some end of the hoper. For instance, on Adrienne Martin's account, hope that p is true is practically rational just in case hoping for p can be incorporated into a schema that advances your rational ends. Brooke could be practically rational in hoping she will earn her college degree despite the difficulty of doing so just in case hoping will help her achieve this or other rational goals, like increasing her knowledge of the world or expanding her social network by remaining in classes. If this is right, then all one needs to have practically rational hope for the happy coincidence is a rational end or ends that would be served by this hope. Anyone already invested in living a moral life would recognize that hope in the happy coincidence staves off despair and thus have practical reason to hope.

This secular response suffers from two problems. The first is a version of the wrong kind of reasons problem (Ebels-Duggan, 2015: 99, Hieronymi, 2005). Whatever consideration justifies an action should count in favor of performing that action directly. When a consideration counts in favor of, say, intending to perform an action but fails to count in favor of performing the action it is the "wrong kind of reason" for that action. Suppose it's true that you will live a morally better life if you hope for the happy coincidence. That fact might give you a reason to try to bring it about that you hope for the happy coincidence, but it doesn't count in favor of the object of your hope – the happy coincidence – at all. The second problem is that hope can be practically rational without being conducive to achieving one's ends. For instance, it is perfectly good for me to hope that my sick friend who lives on another continent gets well even if it makes no difference to any of my activities and goals. The proposed account of the practical rationality of hope, one that supports the secular theory, thus seems wanting.

The theist can then show that a particular kind of religious conviction uniquely supports hope in the happy coincidence of virtue and happiness. The first step is to posit a "moral orderer" – that is, an agent with the power to bring about the hoped-for outcome and the benevolence to be motivated to act providentially. In this part of the argument, the Kantian makes explicit the criteria a divine being must meet in order to play the role of the moral orderer, and the gods of certain theisms are ruled out. The divinity in Stoicism does not play this role, nor a God who owes nothing to human beings for their behavior or who is not required to promote human wellbeing.

Kantians have claimed that the God of the Christian tradition – a God revealed to be engaged in human redemption from evil and sin – fits the bill of the moral orderer. (Of course, not every variety of Christianity accepts that God's power enables God to do this sort of ordering. For example, on a Molinist picture where the optimal antecedents of counterfactuals of freedom for all humans aren't compossible, it could be that God must create a world in which certain persons don't have the opportunities in which they would have freely chosen to perform actions that would have cultivated virtue.)

The next step is to establish the rationality of hope in God as the moral orderer. To do this, we have to maintain, for one, that belief in God is something that can be neither proven nor disproved. It is necessarily uncertain, and so there isn't even the possibility of gaining new evidence that would move the epistemic probability of God's existence to 1 or 0 in this life. This secures and stabilizes the epistemic rationality of hope in God. Further, we can have practical reasons to hope in providential moral ordering that don't suffer the same problems as the secular practical reasons we explored above. For the reason for hope – the possibility that a providential God does reward the virtuous – actually does support the content of the hope in the right way. It needn't contribute instrumentally to my being moral. I might be motivated to be moral by a hope that I'll be rewarded in the afterlife, but in fact this wouldn't provide me with a genuinely good will. It would turn my happiness into an incentive to act rightly, in which case I do not act for the sake of duty but for the sake of happiness. Rather, the hope serves to stabilize my already good will by staving off despair, not as a positive instrument for moral motivation.

4.2.3 Providence and Moral Motivation

Another practical argument that is supposed to count in favor of theism is what John Hare has called the Argument from Providence. Like the previous argument, it takes its inspiration from Kant's discussion of hope in God, and it aims to show that a condition of the possibility of some important practical moral attitude is a kind of assent to theism. Unlike the previous argument, the Argument from Providence takes the chief problem we face to be the rational instability of the motivation to be moral. It maintains that we have to believe in God as providential in order to stabilize moral motivation.

The argument begins by observing that certain anthropological and empirical facts threaten to destabilize morality (Hare, 2015). The pertinent anthropological fact is that we are embodied animals by nature and so have bodily appetites and needs. It follows from this that our happiness, namely the satisfaction of our desires, will inevitably include the satisfaction of our bodily needs and inclinations. We are also rational beings, and qua rational being our end is to achieve moral perfection using reason. The pertinent empirical fact is that when we achieve our rational end, nature hardly seems to reward us with happiness.

(1) Human beings are "creatures of sense and need."
(2) Human happiness requires the satisfaction of our needs and inclinations.
(3) As *rational* animals, we can't live the best kind of human life without having achieved the end of both our rational and animal natures – both moral perfection *and* happiness.
(4) The achievement of moral perfection doesn't typically coincide with the achievement of happiness.

These facts generate a problem:

(5) Unless we rationally believe the natural order will reward moral perfection with happiness, we lack rationally stable motivation to be moral.

The underlying assumption required to move from (4) to (5) is about what Talbot Brewer has called the duality of practical reason (Brewer, 2009). The idea, prevalent among the British moral philosophers from Samuel Clarke and Thomas Hobbes onward, is that practical rationality has two competing aims: our own happiness and the happiness of all. And the natural world is set up in such a way that these inevitably conflict. Therefore, practical reason can't reliably point us in the direction of both aims consistently.

Hare goes on to argue that the *only* way to stabilize the rational motivation to be moral and to achieve the best kind of human life is to believe in a providential God. This God ensures that nature eventually satisfies the needs and inclinations of those who do their moral duty.

(6) Belief in a providential God who rewards moral perfection with happiness gives a person a stable practical reason to be moral.

Hare adds a divine command theoretic twist, namely that "we have to recognize our duties as God's commands, because it is only if they are God's commands that we can rationally believe in the real possibility of the highest good, which is the end that morality itself gives us" (Hare, 2015: 8). So the final part of the argument goes:

(7) Belief in this kind of providential God requires that we believe our moral duties are God's commands.
(8) Therefore, belief in a providential God whose commands constitute our moral duties provides rationally stable moral motivation.

The theism required for the Argument from Providence is thicker than that required for the first Kantian argument. For consider all the further claims we must make about God to endorse the second part of the argument. God must reveal the moral law via divine commands; God's will must be not only consistent with the moral law but exhaustive of it; God's commands must be recognizable as such – not something we merely believe in the content of without awareness that they are divine commands (*pace* Evans, 2014).

Again, not every Christian theism will fit neatly within this schema so as to be able to make use of the Argument from Providence. For some Christian theists hold the view that morality is not exhausted by divine commands, but partly consists in conventional principles generated by human agreement. Additionally, God speaks to humans very differently based on their background experiences on some Christian views (Rea, 2018). This would present a problem if God's commands are supposed to be moral commands and morality is universal in the strong sense, for God's commands on those views are not universal. Finally, on a Thomistic picture the rationality of moral motivation wouldn't be undercut by not recognizing the content of the moral law as coming from divine law; it can be undergirded by belief in the transcendental good.

4.2.4 The Argument from Grace

One final Kantian argument supports theism on the grounds that it uniquely explains how we can act morally. This argument, owing to Hare's interpretation of Kant, is called the Argument from Grace. Like the other Kantian arguments it requires a conception of God familiar to the Christian tradition in several respects.

The Argument from Grace assumes, as a starting point, that human beings naturally prioritize our own happiness over duty. But to be moral, we have to rank duty above happiness, an apparent impossibility for beings like us. If ought implies can, it would seem to follow that the demand of morality is incoherent, requiring us to do something of which we are incapable.

Again, the Kantian solution, according to Hare, appeals to God. We can overcome our natural tendency through divine grace. As Hare points out, "While 'ought' implies 'can,' 'ought' does not imply 'can by our own devices'," and so an appeal to God's assistance allows us to avoid violating the ought implies can principle (Hare, 2015: 13).

This argument requires not belief or hope in God, but instead the metaphysical truth that God does exist and assists humans in acting morally. The conception of God at work is a providential God active in this world, not just in ordering the afterlife. We can imagine God intervening either with the natural order to make moral action easier based on circumstances, or with human psychology to make it easier to be motivated to be moral. The theisms on which God regularly interferes with nature, or on which God is a spirit that can dwell in or possess humans will be able to make use of this argument more naturally than those on which God is aloof from human affairs.

5 Conclusions

In reviewing major arguments regarding the relationship between God and morality in contemporary philosophy, we've heard a subtle theme playing in the background. The theme is that we can operate on very few assumptions about what God is like and conclude quite a lot about theism's relationship to morality. I have been using the term "thin traditional theism" to refer to the minimal account of God that is supposed to serve as a placeholder in these arguments. The advantage of proceeding using thin theism, purportedly, is that a theist in any of the major western religious traditions or who adheres to the omniGod thesis should be able to make use of the arguments.

While I haven't tried to give a knockdown argument against using thin traditional theism in this way (as the view to beat, defend, or draw metaethical implications from), I have tried to unsettle our confidence that doing so will be fruitful. A least-common-denominator kind of theism doesn't show much promise for providing real direction in our thinking about fundamental moral questions. My reason for pessimism arises from the *cumulative case* I have made against the arguments that use thin traditional theism as a starting point or target. We have seen that most (if not all) aren't compelling without additional substantive assumptions about divine attributes or action. So, if these arguments represent philosophy's best attempts to do without substantive theistic assumptions, and my evaluations are on track, then it seems unlikely that we'll make much philosophical progress on questions about God and morality while operating only on the assumption that thin traditional theism is true or false.

It should come as no surprise if it turns out that the labels "theism" and "atheism" fail to carve at the right philosophical joints; for while in other areas of philosophy, a general view often emerges before specific versions of that view, this is not the case with theism and atheism. For instance, foundationalism about epistemic justification splinters off into classical foundationalism, phenomenal conservatism, externalist and internalist varieties. Theism and atheism, however, are importantly different in that, long before philosophers self-identified as theists, there were Jews, polytheists, Hindus, Christians,

Muslims, pantheists, Daoists, and so on. And for any given culture, those who self-identified as atheists were those who rejected the traditional god or gods of that culture (like Socrates, who was obviously a believer in the divine, but charged with a kind of godlessness for not expressing commitment to the mainstream divinities). We have since categorized the beliefs of Muslims, Jews, and Christians as falling under the genus of traditional theism based on expression of faith in a singular divine entity.

Some categorizations are more useful for certain purposes than others, and what I am suggesting is that traditional theism and atheism are not the most useful categories for moral philosophical inquiry. Here's an analogy: we could group organisms based on the number of feet they have, with the result that humans are in the same group as birds, amphibians and dinosaurs with cats and dogs, snakes with fish, and so on. Biologists, though, opt for the taxonomy that groups humans with dogs and cats, snakes with dinosaurs, fish and amphibians on their own because, as things turn out, whether something has a spine or is warm blooded or uses external reproduction matters much more for answering the biologist's questions. As things turn out, whether there is an all-powerful being that is loving towards humans in a particular sort of way or not, or whether some power directs evolutionary development to produce truth-tracking cognitive structures in us or not – these sorts of distinctions are the ones that matter for answering the moral philosopher's questions.

Thus, a more promising method of inquiry is to work out how particular theisms or their denial relate to metaethical positions. We should take an approach similar to the philosopher of physics who starts from theories scientists endorse or which can be derived from observing their practices, and extracts the implications of those theories. The conditionalizing move ("If theory x is correct, what follows?") is a move that sets apart philosophy of physics from theoretical physics, and similarly it can set apart philosophical theistic ethics from theology.

In concluding, I want to consider two objections to this alternative method, then gesture at some recent work that exemplifies what I think we should be up to.

5.1 Too-Thick Theism?

The first objection is that what I propose requires that we assume too much about what God is like to be philosophy. It would be, as Robert Adams puts it, religious ethics. And we should leave this to the theologians. Philosophers ought to rely on as few claims as are needed to draw their conclusions. We should rely on as thin a conception of theism as is necessary for establishing metaethical claims; otherwise, we make our metaethical views too expensive for anyone who hasn't already bought into theism.

This worry is somewhat misguided. Our evaluations of the prominent arguments show that more theistic assumptions are necessary to draw the metaethical conclusions that are supposed to follow. In light of this, we would seem to have two options: backing off completely and admitting that theism makes no difference to answers to metaethical questions, or owning the further theistic assumptions the arguments require.

A practical benefit of following the implications of thick theism is that it allows philosophy to make closer contact with people's lived religious experiences. A Sufi might be curious as to what moral beliefs would be licensed by her particular mysticism but no other forms of Islam; or a protestant Christian might want to know, before converting to Catholicism, whether this should have any bearing on her beliefs about fundamental moral truths. Philosophical arguments that make explicit what certain theistic commitments logically entail or probabilify would be helpful for people earnestly seeking for these kinds of answers. In general, the God our friends, neighbors, students, and colleagues believe in or don't is a God under some substantive description or other – the God who led Israel out of Egypt, or the God who commanded us to love our enemies, or the God who allowed their child to die young or their home country to spend decades in civil war. When these people seek answers to fundamental moral questions as they relate to God, perhaps they are better served when we start with the thick conceptions of a God they already trust or doubt, worship or fear.

5.2 Exclusivism

The second objection to my proposal raises a practical concern. Won't this lead to exclusivist philosophy? It may well drive theists of varying traditions apart, rather than helping them find common ground. If the Sufi examines the implications of her beliefs for metaethics, the Catholic does the same, and so on, we will have created even more silos within philosophy of religion and moral philosophy than already exist! If the alternative method of inquiry led to these consequences, that would be grounds for skepticism about the fruitfulness of method.

Already, however, we've had to think more carefully about many religious traditions and differences between them. Rather than working with general characterizations that could quickly become caricatures of a view, we have needed to examine more fine-grained pictures of God from within a variety of faith traditions – Shi'ite Islam, Orthodox Judaism, apophatic Christianity, open theism, for example. Like the philosopher of physics who does well to study in detail and compare multiple theories, moral philosophers and philosophers of religion will need to consider with care and precision the views of God held by others, whether like or unlike her own views, in order to figure out where they lead in terms of metaethical claims. Exploring the implications of thick religious commitments will likely lead to deeper engagement with a variety of traditions than is currently the norm.

In fact, the alternative way of proceeding could have quite the opposite effect from siloing. In introducing thick varieties of theism to the discussion we may learn that some theisms have more in common with certain secular outlooks, when it comes to the fundamental moral questions, than they do with other theisms. An orthodox Jewish theist, or a theist who believes the divine motivation theory, might be an unlikely ally with a contemporary Humean, while a Catholic theist has more in common with the naturalist Aristotelian when it comes to metaethics than with the orthodox Jew.

5.3 Some Exemplars

Marilynn Adams, in her seminal work *Christ and Horrors*, takes the sort of approach I suggest we use. She presents a moral problem – that evils in this world threaten to destroy the meaningfulness of human life – and considers what God must be like – in particular, what the nature of second person of the Trinity must be like – for this problem to have a satisfying solution (Adams, 2006). While acknowledging a place for natural philosophical theology (arguments that are available to all reasonable persons without any revelation) she argues that the dominance of the "least-common-denominator" approach leads to a thinning out, stripping symbols of God and Christ so thoroughly that little motivation is left to hold a religious ethics rather than a secular one (ibid.: 6).

Adams resists the trend and instead uses a coherentist methodology, according to which "human reason's best chance at truth is won through the effort of integrating our data with our many and diverse intuitions into a coherent picture with the theoretical virtues of clarity, consistency, explanatory woes, and fruitfulness" (ibid.: 11). This method allows for there to be multiple rational alternatives with different starting points, and for us to explore them in a philosophical frame of mind. She starts with Christian doctrines about Christ as a starting point, as well as the data about the ruinous effects of evil on meaningful human life. The task, then, is "to re-present robust Christology as a viable competitor in the market place of religious and theological worldviews" using philosophical arguments that show how Christ's life can explain the salvation of humans from final destruction by ruinous evils.

An example of a comparative project in theistic ethics is Mariam Al-Attar's *Islamic Ethics*. Al-Attar's project explores questions about the source and nature of morality in various strands of Arabo-Islamic thought (al-Attar, 2012). In part, the need for such a project arises from the widespread assumption that an ethics supported by Islamic tradition and texts must be a certain form of divine voluntarism, and perhaps one with negative socio-political consequences (ibid.: xii). But Mu'tazilites in the ninth century challenged the idea that moral goodness or badness reduced to divine commands exclusively (ibid.: ch. 4). Al-Attar's contemporary philosophical discussion of Islamic ethics, with its detailed account of the relationships of certain ideas to historical developments in the tradition and sacred texts, provides an accurate picture of the way those particular theistic beliefs play out on the metaethical stage, and a corrective for many commonplace assumptions about Islamic ethics.

We can also learn from an exemplar who takes the advice in the opposite direction, not working from within a particular theistic tradition, but bringing to the table a variety of theism not usually discussed *because* it does not fit the mold of traditional theism. Gerald Harrison constructs an abductive argument for an innovative theistic account of normative reasons that assumes not even the OmniGod thesis: divine psychologism. Harrison works out a description of god from the idea of what we would need a being to look like to support a theory of normative reasons. The argument of the book runs: Normative reasons are favoring relations; favoring relations are only found in a mind; but as normative reasons are not just any type of favoring relations but objective favoring relations, they must be external to us; they must exhibit a certain kind of unity, and so need to be in a single mind. It follows that normative reasons are found in a single external mind, which we may call god (Harrison 2018). Harrison's argument has a moral corollary akin to the Argument from Objective Moral Value. If moral reasons or values are a species of normative reasons, or grounded in normative reasons as the buck-passing account of value suggests, then they too depend on god – an external, unified mind. One could also run a parallel argument based on the objectivity of moral value: value is only objective if it is unified and external to us; but value is, conceptually, something that is conferred on something by being valued; thus objective moral value must come from an external mind that can confer value – call this god.[3] Right now, nontraditional conceptions of God

---

[3] Thanks to an anonymous referee for pointing out Harrison's work.

are beginning to enter discussions in the metaphysical and epistemological strands of philosophy of religion. Perhaps it is time for them to have a seat at the metaethical and ethical table.

The example with which I'll draw my discussion to a close takes seriously one thick theism and its attendant *practices,* and aims to give a philosophical account of how those practices relate to moral life. Terence Cuneo's *Ritualized Faith* homes in on a particular faith – Eastern Orthodox Christianity (Cuneo, 2016). Cuneo attempts to answer the question of why this faith includes an injunction to perform certain practices, namely, the reenactment of the events of Holy Week by the congregation. His reply articulates several ways that this particular practice of reenactment affects the moral life of the participants, in general by aiding them to create a narrative identity and achieve certain moral ideals. For instance, some of the speech acts performed while reading the biblical narrative have the effect of making the speaker similar to the characters in the narrative by prompting the speaker to perform, say, an act of confession. When the performer reads the narrative with certain intentions and desires, the "imitation, in this case, begets identification" (ibid.: 100). Sometimes, identification is a necessary step on the road to achieving a moral ideal; confession, for example, may be a necessary step in the process of becoming a forgiving person. In that case, the ritual act contributes to the person's moral life by helping her to perform the action necessary for achieving the ideal.

Toward the end of the chapter, Cuneo makes a further move that illustrates the kind of results we can get from doing substantive theistic ethics like this. The discussion leads us to ponder a general normative question of general interest, even outside this particular religious tradition, but which hasn't received attention from philosophers: namely, whether there is any distinctive contribution to the moral life made by the speech acts performed in liturgy due to the kind of background commitments and social context. Might this contribution differ from that made by, say, performing a part in a play or reading a novel aloud alone?

Exploring the ethical implications and questions that arise for thick theisms could bring us to questions of this sort, questions contemporary philosophers may not have spent much time writing about but which are important for our understanding the fine contours of the moral life.

References

Adams, M. M. (2006). *Christ and Horrors: The Coherence of Christology*. Cambridge, UK; New York: Cambridge University Press.

(2008). *Horrendous Evils and the Goodness of God*. Ithaca: Cornell University Press.

Adams, R. M. (1999). *Finite and Infinite Goods: A Framework for Ethics*. New York: Oxford University Press.

Almeida, M. J., & Oppy, G. (2003). Sceptical Theism and Evidential Arguments from Evil. *Australasian Journal of Philosophy, 81*(4), 496–516. https://doi .org/10.1080/713659758

al-Attar, M. (2012). *Islamic Ethics: Divine Command Theory in Arabo-Islamic Thought*. New York; London: Routledge.

Anscombe, G. E. M. (1958). Modern Moral Philosophy. *Philosophy, 33*, 1–19.

Attridge, H. (2009). Wolterstorff, Rights, Wrongs, and the Bible. *Journal of Religious Ethics, 37*(2), 209–20.

Bedke, M. (2009). Intuitive Non-Naturalism Meets Cosmic Coincidence. Pacific Philosophical Quarterly *90*(2), 188–209.

Bergmann, M. (2001). Skeptical Theism and Rowe's New Evidential Argument from Evil. *Nous, 35*(2), 278–296. https://doi.org/10.1111/0029-4624.00297

(2012). Common Sense Skeptical Theism. In *Science, Religion, and Metaphysics*. Michael Rea & Kelly Clark (Eds.). Oxford: Oxford University Press.

(2014). Skeptical Theism, Atheism, and Total Evidence Skepticism. In *Skeptical Theism: New Essays*. Trent Dougherty & Justin McBrayer (Eds.). Oxford: Oxford University Press.

Bergmann, M., Murray, M. J., & Rea, M. C. (eds.). (2011). *Divine Evil? The Moral Character of the God of Abraham*. Oxford; New York: Oxford University Press.

Bergmann, M., & Rea, M. (2005). In Defence of Sceptical Theism: A Reply to Almeida and Oppy. *Australasian Journal of Philosophy, 83*(2), 241–251. https://doi.org/10.1080/00048400500111147

Blackman, Reid. (forthcoming). Nietzsche's Repudiation of Guilt. In B. Cokelet & C. Maley (Eds.), *The Moral Psychology of Guilt*. London: Rowman & Littlefield.

Bogardus, T. (2016). Only All Naturalists Should Worry About Only One Evolutionary Debunking Argument. *Ethics, 126*(3), 636–661. https://doi .org/10.1086/684711

Brewer, T. (2009). *The Retrieval of Ethics*. Oxford; New York: Oxford University Press.

Brody, B. (1981). Morality and Religion Reconsidered. In P. Helm (Ed.), *Divine Commands and Morality*. Oxford; New York: Oxford University Press.

Chignell, A. (2014). Rational Hope, Possibility, and Divine Action. In *Religion within the Bounds of Mere Reason: A Critical Guide* (pp. 98–117). Cambridge: Cambridge University Press.

Cockayne, J. (2018). The Dark Knight of the Soul: Weaning and the Problem of Divine Withdrawal. *Religious Studies*, *54*(1), 73–90. https://doi.org/10.1017/S0034412516000366

Cottingham, J. (2005). *The Spiritual Dimension: Religion, Philosophy, and Human Value*. Cambridge, UK; New York: Cambridge University Press.

Craig, W. L., & Kurtz, P. (2009). The Kurtz/Craig Debate. In R. K. Garcia & N. L. King (Eds.), *Is Goodness without God Good Enough? A Debate on Faith, Secularism, and Ethics*. Lanham: Rowman & Littlefield.

Craig, W. L., & Sinnott-Armstrong, W. (2004). *God? A Debate between a Christian and an Atheist*. Oxford; New York: Oxford University Press.

Cudworth, R. (1996). *A Treatise Concerning Eternal and Immutable Morality*. (S. Hutton, Ed.). New York; Cambridge: Cambridge University Press.

Cuneo, T. (2016). *Ritualized Faith: Essays on the Philosophy of Liturgy*. New York: Oxford University Press.

Danaher, J. (2017). In Defence of the Epistemological Objection to Divine Command Theory. Sophia. https://doi.org/10.1007/s11841-017-0622-9

Darwall, S. L. (1995). *The British Moralists and the Internal "Ought", 1640–1740*. Cambridge; New York: Cambridge University Press.

Davidson, M. (1999). A Demonstration Against Theistic Activism. *Religious Studies*, *35*(3), 277–290. https://doi.org/10.1017/S0034412599004886

Davies, B. (2006). *The Reality of God and the Problem of Evil*. London: Continuum.

Deng, N. (2018). Eternity in Christian Thought. In E. N. Zalta (Ed.), *The Stanford Encyclopedia of Philosophy* (Fall 2018). https://plato.stanford.edu/archives/fall2018/entries/eternity/

Draper, P. (1996). The Skeptical Theist. In D. Howard-Snyder (Ed.), *The Evidential Argument from Evil*. Bloomington: Indiana University Press.

Ebels-Duggan, K. (2015). The Right, the Good, and the Threat of Despair: (Kantian) Ethics and the Need for Hope in God. In J. L. Kvanvig (Ed.), *Oxford Studies in Philosophy of Religion* (Vol.7, pp. 81–110).

Emon, A. M. (2010). *Islamic Natural Law Theories*. New York: Oxford University Press.

Enoch, D. (2007). An Outline of an Argument for Robust Metanormative Realism. In R. Shafer-Landau (Ed.), *Oxford Studies in Metaethics* (Vol.2, pp. 21–48). New York: Oxford University Press.

Evans, C. S. (2014). *God and Moral Obligation*. Oxford: Oxford University Press.

(2018). Moral Arguments for the Existence of God. In E. N. Zalta (Ed.), *The Stanford Encyclopedia of Philosophy* (Fall 2018 Edition). Retrieved from https://plato.stanford.edu/archives/fall2018/entries/moral-arguments-god/

Fisher, J. (2001). The Theology of Dis/similarity: Negation in Pseudo-Dionysius. *The Journal of Religion, 81*(4), 529–548. https://doi.org/10.1086/490935

Fitzpatrick, W. (2015). Debunking Evolutionary Debunking of Ethical Realism. Philosophical Studies, *172*(4), 883–904.

Hare, J. E. (2015). *God's Command* (1st edn.). Oxford: Oxford University Press.

Harrison, G. K. (2018). *Normative Reasons and Theism*. Cham: Palgrave Macmillan. https://doi.org/10.1007/978-3-319-90796-3

Heathwood, C. (2017). Could Morality Have a Source? *Journal of Ethics and Social Philosophy, 6*(2), 1–20. https://doi.org/10.26556/jesp.v6i2.62

Hendrickson, W. A., & Ward, K. B. (1975). Atomic Models for the Polypeptide Backbones of Myohemerythrin and Hemerythrin. *Biochemical and Biophysical Research Communications, 66*(4), 1349–1356.

Hieronymi, P. (2005). The Wrong Kind of Reason. *Journal of Philosophy, 102*(9), 437–457. https://doi.org/10.5840/jphil2005102933

Hoover, J. (2007). *Ibn Taymiyya's Theodicy of Perpetual Optimism*. Leiden: Brill.

Ichikawa, J. (2011). Quantifiers, Knowledge, and Counterfactuals. *Philosophy and Phenomenological Research, 82*(2), 287–313. https://doi.org/10.1111/j.1933-1592.2010.00427.x

Jacobs, J. D. (2015 The Ineffable, Inconceivable, and Incomprehensible God: Fundamentality and Apophatic Theology. In J. L. Kvanvig (Ed.), *Oxford Studies in Philosophy of Religion* (Vol. 6, pp.158–176).

Jeffrey, A. (2015). *On the Moral Significance of Conscience*. Dissertation, Washington, DC. http://hdl.handle.net/10822/761505

Jeffrey, A. (forthcoming). A Thomistic Account of Conscience and Guilt. In B. Cokelet & C. Maley (Eds.), *The Moral Psychology of Guilt*. London: Rowman & Littlefield.

(2015). On the Moral Significance of Conscience (Doctoral Dissertation). Retrieved from Georgetown University Institutional Repository: Graduate Theses and Dissertations. (Accession no. 2015-09-11T19:25:08Z)

Jonas, H. (1987). The Concept of God after Auschwitz: A Jewish Voice. *The Journal of Religion, 67*(1), 1–13. https://doi.org/10.1086/487483

Jordan, J. (2006). Does Skeptical Theism Lead to Moral Skepticism? *Philosophy and Phenomenological Research, 72*(2), 403–417. https://doi.org/10.1111/j.1933-1592.2006.tb00567.x

Joyce, R. (2001). *The Myth of Morality*. Cambridge: Cambridge University Press.

Korman, D., & Locke, D. (2020). Against Minimalist Responses to Moral Debunking Arguments. In *Oxford Studies in Metaethics* (Vol. 15). Oxford: Oxford University Press.

Legenhausen, G. (1986). Is God a Person? *Religious Studies, 22*(3–4), 307. https://doi.org/10.1017/S0034412500018345

Lewis, C. S. (1952). Mere Christianity. New York: Harper Collins.

Lisska, A. J. (1998). *Aquinas's Theory of Natural Law: An Analytic Reconstruction.* Oxford: Clarendon Press.

Lord, E. (2018). *The Importance of Being Rational*. New York: Oxford University Press.

Lott, M. (2018). Must Realists Be Skeptics? An Aristotelian Reply to a Darwinian Dilemma. *Philosophical Studies 175*(1),71–96.

Mackie, J. L. (1955). Evil and Omnipotence. *Mind, 64*, 200–212.

(1973). *Ethics: Inventing Right and Wrong*. London: Penguin Books.

McBrayer, J. P., & Swenson, P. (2012). Scepticism about the Argument from Divine Hiddenness. *Religious Studies, 48*(2), 129–150. https://doi.org/10.1017/S003441251100014X

McGinnis, J. (2015). The Hiddenness of "Divine Hiddenness": Divine Love in Medieval Islamic Lands. In A. Green & E. Stump (Eds.), *Hidden Divinity and Religious Belief: New Perspectives*. Cambridge: Cambridge University Press.

McPherson, T. (2011). Against Quietist Normative Realism. *Philosophical Studies, 154*(2), 223–240. https://doi.org/10.1007/s11098-010-9535-y

Miller, C. (2013). The Euthyphro Dilemma. *Blackwell International Encyclopedia of Ethics*: 1–7.

Milona, M. (2018). Finding Hope. Canadian Journal of Philosophy, 1–20. https://doi.org/10.1080/00455091.2018.1435612

Morton, J. (ms). Can Theists Avoid Epistemological Objections to Moral (and Normative) Realism?

Moon, A. (2017). Plantinga's Religious Epistemology, Skeptical Theism, and Debunking Arguments. *Faith and Philosophy, 34*(4), 449–470.

Morriston, W. (2009) The Moral Obligations of Reasonable Non-believers. *International Journal for Philosophy of Religion, 65* (1), 1–20.

(2012). God and the Ontological Foundation of Morality. *Religious Studies, 48* (1), 15–34.

Morton, J. (2018). When Do Replies to the Evolutionary Debunking Argument Against Moral Realism Beg the Question? Australasian Journal of Philosophy, 1–16. https://doi.org/10.1080/00048402.2018.1455718

Morton, J., & Sampson, E. (2014). Parsimony and the Argument from Queerness. *Res Philosophica*, *91*(4), 609–627. https://doi.org/10.11612/resphil .2014.91.4.4

Murphy, M. C. (1998). Divine Command, Divine Will, and Moral Obligation. *Faith and Philosophy*, *15*(1), 3–27. https://doi.org/10.5840/faithphil 19981512

(2002). *An Essay on Divine Authority*. Ithaca: Cornell University Press.

(2011). *God and Moral Law: On the Theistic Explanation of Morality*. Oxford; New York: Oxford University Press.

(2014). Perfect Goodness. The Stanford Encyclopedia of Philosophy (Summer 2014 Edition). Edward N. Zalta (ed.), https://plato.stanford.edu /archives/spr2014/entries/perfect-goodness/.

(2017). *God's Own Ethics: Norms of Divine Agency and the Argument from Evil*. Oxford; New York: Oxford University Press.

Nagasawa, Y. (2018). The Problem of Evil for Atheists. In N. N. Trakakis (Ed.), *The Problem of Evil: Eight Views in Dialogue* (pp. 151–175). Oxford: Oxford University Press.

Trakakis, N., & Nagasawa, Y. (2004). Skeptical Theism and Moral Skepticism: A Reply to Almeida and Oppy. *Ars Disputandi*, *4*(1), 222–228. https://doi .org/10.1080/15665399.2004.10819851

Nielson, K. (1973). *Ethics Without God*. Buffalo: Prometheus Books.

O'Donovan, O. (2009). The Language of Rights and Conceptual History. *Journal of Religious Ethics*, *37*(2), 193–208.

Olson, J. (2011). In Defense of Moral Error Theory. In M. Brady (Ed.), *New Waves in Metaethics* (pp. 62–84). London: Palgrave Macmillan UK. https://doi.org/10.1057/9780230294899_4

Padgett, A. (1992). *God, Eternity and the Nature of Time*. London: Macmillan.

Peels, R. (2016). Can God Repent? In J. L. Kvanvig (Ed.), *Oxford Studies in Philosophy of Religion* (Vol. 7, pp. 190–212). Oxford: Oxford University Press.

Pessin, S. (2013). Ibn Gabirol's Theology of Desire. Cambridge: Cambridge University Press.

Plantinga, A. (1965). The Free Will Defense. In Max Black (Ed.), *Philosophy in America* (pp. 204–220). Ithaca: Cornell University Press.

(2011). Content and Natural Selection. *Philosophy and Phenomenological Research*, *83*(2), 435–458. https://doi.org/10.1111/j.1933-1592 .2010.00444.x

Quinn, P. L. (1978). *Divine Commands and Moral Requirements*. Oxford: Clarendon Press.

(1990). The Recent Revival of Divine Command Ethics. *Philosophy and Phenomenological Research, 50*: 345. https://doi.org/10.2307/2108047

Rachels, J. (1971). God and Human Attitudes. *Religious Studies, 7*(4), 325–337.

Rea, M. C. (2013). Skeptical Theism and the "Too-Much-Skepticism" Objection. In J. P. McBrayer & D. Howard-Snyder (Eds.), *The Blackwell Companion to the Problem of Evil* (pp. 482–506). Malden: Wiley-Blackwell.

(2018). *The Hiddenness of God*. Oxford; New York: Oxford University Press.

Rosen, G. (2003). Culpability and Ignorance. *Proceedings of the Aristotelian Society 103*(1), 61–84. https://doi.org/10.1111/j.0066-7372.2003.00064.x

Rowe, W. (1996). The Evidential Argument from Evil: A Second Look. In D. Howard-Snyder (Ed.), *The Evidential Argument from Evil* (pp. 262-285). Bloomington: Indiana University Press.

Rutledge, J. C. (2017). Commonsense, Skeptical Theism, and Different Sorts of Closure of Inquiry Defeat. In *Faith and Philosophy, 34*(1), 17–32. https://doi.org/10.5840/faithphil201712576

Scanlon, T. M. (1998). *What We Owe to Each Other*. Cambridge: Belknap Press.

Schellenberg, J. L. (2015). *The Hiddenness Argument: Philosophy's New Challenge to Belief in God*. Oxford: Oxford University Press.

Setiya, K. (2012). *Knowing Right from Wrong*. Oxford: Oxford University Press.

Shafer-Landau, R. (2009). A Defence of Categorical Reasons. *Proceedings of the Aristotelian Society, 109*, 189–206. https://doi.org/10.1111/j.1467-9264.2009.00264.x

Shoemaker, D. (2000). Reductionist Contractualism: Moral Motivation and the Expanding Self. Canadian Journal of Philosophy, *30*(3), 334–370. https://doi.org/10.1080/00455091.2000.10717536

Simmons, J. A. (2011). *God and the Other: Ethics and Politics after the Theological Turn*. Bloomington: Indiana University Press.

Sinclair, N. (2011). The Explanationist Argument for Moral Realism. *Canadian Journal of Philosophy, 41*(1), 1–24. https://doi.org/10.1353/cjp.2011.0005

Sinnott-Armstrong, W. (2009). *Morality without God?* Oxford; New York: Oxford University Press.

Street, S. (2006). A Darwinian Dilemma for Realist Theories of Value. *Philosophical Studies, 127*, 109–166.

Stump, E. (2010). *Wandering in Darkness: Narrative and the Problem of Suffering*. Oxford: Oxford University Press.

Stump, E. and Green, A. (2015). Hidden Divinity and Religious Belief. Cambridge: Cambridge University Press.

Tennyson, A. L. (1851). In Memoriam. Boston: Knight and Millet.

Wainwright, W. J. (2005). *Religion and Morality*. Burlington, VT: Ashgate.

Warmke, B. (2017). God's Standing to Forgive: *Faith and Philosophy, 34*(4), 381–402. https://doi.org/10.5840/faithphil201711690

Westphal, M. (2001). Overcoming Ontotheology. New York: Fordham University Press.

Wielenberg, E. J. (2010). On the Evolutionary Debunking of Morality. *Ethics, 120*(3), 441–464. https://doi.org/10.1086/652292

   (2014) *Robust Ethics: The Metaphysics and Epistemology of Godless Normative Realism*. Oxford: Oxford University Press.

Wolterstorff, N. (2008). Justice: Rights and Wrongs. Princeton: Princeton University Press.

Zagzebski, L. T. (2013). *Omnisubjectivity: A Defense of a Divine Attribute*. Milwaukee, Wisconsin: Marquette University Press.

Acknowledgments

The University of South Alabama provided a Support and Development grant for a workshop on the manuscript that proved helpful at the final stage. I owe special gratitude to Terence Cuneo, Kyla Ebels-Duggan, and Mark Murphy for spending three days in conversation about the core arguments and ideas at the workshop. I am also grateful to Samuel Baker, Mike Bergmann, Chris Dodsworth, Alli Krile Thornton, Kevin Meeker, Mike Rea, Alex Whalen, participants of the 2018 Women in Philosophy of Religion Workshop in San Diego, and participants of the 2018 Innsbruck Summer Seminar in Analytic Theology for their thoughtful discussion of earlier drafts.

Cambridge Elements ≡

Philosophy of Religion

Yujin Nagasawa

University of Birmingham

Yujin Nagasawa is Professor of Philosophy and Co-Director of the John Hick Centre for Philosophy of Religion at the University of Birmingham. He is currently President of the British Society for the Philosophy of Religion. He is a member of the Editorial Board of Religious Studies, the International Journal for Philosophy of Religion and Philosophy Compass.

About the Series

This Cambridge Elements series provides concise and structured introductions to all the central topics in the philosophy of religion. It offers balanced, comprehensive coverage of multiple perspectives in the philosophy of religion. Contributors to the series are cutting-edge researchers who approach central issues in the philosophy of religion. Each provides a reliable resource for academic readers and develops new ideas and arguments from a unique viewpoint.

Cambridge Elements ☰

Philosophy of Religion

Printed in the United States
By Bookmasters